About the Authors

Gill Hines is an educator with a huge amount of experience. She has worked with many parents, young people and teachers, offering workshops, mentoring and support for a wide variety of issues for over 35 years. Dr Alison Baverstock is an academic, author and mother of four, who met Gill through participation in one of her workshops. Both are regularly interviewed in the media about parenting, families and issues to do with young people. Their previous books together are *Whatever! A Down-to-earth Guide to Parenting Teenagers* and *It's Not Fair! Parenting the Bright and Challenging Child* (both Piatkus). This new title also features the hugely popular case studies and question-and-answer sections of the earlier books.

Advance Praise for *Later!*

'*Later!* is essential reading for any of us who confront the reality of moving on; in entertaining style, it helps us to look at the realities of the changing nature of our family lives. With simple and amusing exercises it both stretches our thinking and allows us to make some sense of the emotional turmoil that change can bring. For professionals and for parents alike this is a book well worth reading.'
Nick Whitfield, Chief Executive, Director of Children's Services, Achieving for Children

'Read this book, absorb its warm wisdom and apply its practical advice and you will without doubt become a better parent and your children better adults. They'll be better prepared for the world that awaits them, and you'll be better prepared for life after they've achieved their independence.'
Dr Steve Carey, DPhil, Clinical Hypnotherapist, Victoria, Australia

'Parenting young adults today is an increasingly tricky business. With so many uncontrollable outside influences coming into play, doubts and dilemmas abound. This book will help you navigate a way through them.

With day-to-day dilemmas explored through meticulously gathered real-life testimonies and case studies, this is no abstract self-help guide. The authors reassure us that we are by no means alone; that there is always someone facing similar – or worse – problems, and that there is more than one "correct" solution to every dilemma.

Later! suggests strategies for coping, while keeping in touch with our own identities. Refreshingly, it also points out that we all do the wrong thing sometimes – and that's OK. It's consistency and loving care that matters and, above all, not giving up.'

Sue Cook, writer and broadcaster

'Can your offspring sew on a button? Do they treat your home like a hotel? Are they in trouble of some sort? Are they coping? Are you coping?

Parenting is a process of constant evolution and, although it brings huge rewards, it is not always easy to negotiate well. With this is mind, the authors of *Later!* have written a wise and practical guide to help parents guide their offspring through the 16–23 stage. The advice is compassionate, realistic, light of touch and unafraid. What better guide could there be?'

Elizabeth Buchan, author and mother of two

'A book full of pragmatic and practical advice that rings bells on every page.'

David Roche, bookseller, publisher, agent and
father of three sons

LATER!

A GUIDE TO PARENTING
A YOUNG ADULT

Gill Hines and Alison Baverstock

with a foreword by Sandi Toksvig

piatkus

PIATKUS

First published in Great Britain in 2014 by Piatkus

A CIP catalogue record for this book
is available from the British Library.

ISBN 978-0-349-40446-2

Authors' Note
The names of all individuals mentioned in this book
have been changed to protect their privacy

Typeset in Stone Serif by M Rules
Printed and bound in Great Britain by
Clays Ltd, St Ives plc

Papers used by Piatkus are from well-managed forests
and other responsible sources.

MIX
Paper from
responsible sources
FSC® C104740

Piatkus
An imprint of
Little, Brown Book Group
100 Victoria Embankment
London EC4Y 0DY

An Hachette UK Company
www.hachette.co.uk

www.piatkus.co.uk

Contents

Acknowledgements

The authors would like to thank a range of colleagues and friends who have read sections of this manuscript, made helpful comments and generally guided its progress. Many of our collaborators have preferred to remain anonymous, but we would particularly like to thank Axel Thill for his help with the money chapter and David Tchilingirian for guidance on nutrition. We are grateful to our publishers, Piatkus, with whom we have now had a long relationship – ever since they first published *Whatever! A Down-to-earth Guide to Parenting Teenagers* in 2005 and *It's Not Fair! Parenting the Bright and Challenging Child* in 2008. This time we would particularly like to thank Anne Lawrance, Grace Mcnary-Winefield, Jillian Stewart and Jan Cutler. Finally, we would like to thank our families for ongoing tolerance and support.

Foreword

'Our youth now love luxury. They have bad manners, contempt for authority; they show disrespect for their elders and love chatter in place of exercise; they no longer rise when elders enter the room; they contradict their parents, chatter before company; gobble up their food and tyrannize their teachers.'

The words of a twenty-first century parent? No, that was Socrates, the classical Greek philosopher writing nearly two and a half thousand years ago. That quote might lead one to think that for generations nothing has really changed when it comes to parenting but, apart from a few broad brushstrokes, I'm not sure it's true. I think the world has changed beyond all measure and with astonishing speed in my lifetime.

In the first flush of parenting, everyone – even those who have never parented – has advice to give to the new mother or father. Some of it is helpful, some is not and some is simply from interfering relatives. I've brought up three kids and I learnt pretty quickly that you can divide early childhood into two distinct phases. The first I call 'scribbling', which is when children use crayons simply to make a mess, and the second is 'colouring within the lines', which is when they have mastered both fine motor skills and a degree of patience. Once you get your offspring into the colouring-in phase then life as a parent improves no end. Your demanding little emperor can be distracted and is even heading towards sensible conversation. I pass this knowledge on to anyone still suffering the scribbling years so that they can see light at the end of the tunnel.

The information no one knew to share with me when my babies were babies was that modern parenting is now a much longer road than our own parents experienced. My first venture into the solo adult world consisted of renting a single room in London for £9 a week, when I was 18. It was a terrible place, where the restless mice and the smell of gas kept me awake at night, but I loved the independence of it. Sadly, the economics of today make even such a step less and less likely for young adults, many of whom continue to live at home out of necessity. It's not easy for them but, dare I say, it is not always a total pleasure for the parents. Much has been made of mothers and fathers suffering from 'empty nest' syndrome but few consider the issues related to a nest that is beginning to feel a little too full. For the parent who watched their child grow up and dreamt of freedom from responsibility, the parent whose car bears a bumper sticker with the words 'Busy spending my kid's inheritance', a child who won't or can't leave home can be tough to deal with.

There are other issues, too. My father passed away the week my oldest daughter was born. That was twenty-five years ago. My dad was a marvellous fellow and gave me some very sound advice: 'never trust a man in a ready-made bow tie', 'don't attend a party without having checked who's in the obituaries' and 'always remember that one martini is not enough, two is plenty but three is too many'. I live by those maxims but I am aware of the possibility that his old words of wisdom would not quite suffice for the next generation. I often think how amazed he would be at how the world has changed. He loved technology but never used a mobile phone because, by the time he died, they were yet to become part of our daily lives.

Today all of us, but particularly young adults, face a constant onslaught from endless, instant communication and the pressure of social media. I am appalled at the number of young people, for example, who wish to have plastic surgery in order to improve their 'online image'. My kids are all in their early twenties and when they were born these were things that never occurred to me I might one day have to consider.

For the modern parent, fresh approaches and negotiations are needed and that's why we need a straight-talking, practical guide like this. It is designed to help parents help their children but there is a twist to it which I like – the authors also remind the mother or the father in the picture not to forget to think about themselves as well. The kids may be appalled.

Later! is a book that will help you assess what kind of parent you are and how you might improve for the sake of both your off-spring and your sanity. It includes practical tips to get your child cooking the odd meal; how to cope with drug issues; when to speak up and when to bite your tongue; dealing with the unexpected; coping with sexual activity (your own and your child's); and knowing when to hold back on giving help, even though it is usually quicker to 'do it myself'.

We could all do with a wise woman sitting in the corner dispensing advice but sadly such delights are rare in a busy world, so this book is a fine substitute. If I incorporate just one or two of the suggestions in here then I know the kids will benefit in the long run. Perhaps they will even respect the parent who tries to improve and will come to repeat the words of the anonymous author who once said, 'When I was a boy of fourteen, my father was so ignorant I could hardly stand to have the old man around. But when I got to be twenty-one, I was astonished at how much he had learned in seven years.'

Sandi Toksvig OBE, writer, broadcaster,
Chancellor – and mother of three

Introduction

One minute you are taking your children to school, the next they are off to a more independent stage in their lives. It may seem like only months since you were first filling their lunch box for primary school, but the school career moves with such momentum that it won't be long before you are suddenly facing life without having them at home on a daily basis.

How do you prepare for a time when your child's excitement at the prospect of leaving school, going to university, finding a job or living on their own can leave you feeling dull, passed by and obsessed by detail that they see as unimportant? How do you start to think about what to do with the rest of *your* life – picking up previous or new ambitions, both personal and professional, and prioritising your own friends and interests?

How do you handle the situation when, as is increasingly common, your children later decide to return home to live – in the process shattering the living arrangements that had developed without them, and creating endless mess as well as volunteering the kind of opinions you had become used to managing without.

Later! is an empathetic and practical guide to making sense of life at a time when all the ground rules need to be reconsidered, if not renegotiated. Packed with strategies for the effective analysis and management of a situation that neither of you has handled before, the authors offer sound thinking and the reassurance that others are feeling the same.

A particular and unique feature of this book is the emphasis on exploring the situation from two different points of view. One is the parent role that you have maintained for so long, but which needs to adapt and change to living with a young adult. The second is the non-parent you, who has been left somewhat in the shade for the last 16–20 years while being Mum or Dad took over. This older, but less familiar, you needs to be nurtured and encouraged in much the same way as your young person.

All the decisions and situations your young person is going through need (re)consideration from your point of view too, but years of busyness in managing their lives, as well as delivering the supporting structure for the family, can leave you unused to thinking about your own needs and priorities. This book considers everyone's hopes and plans – in the process, offering everyone the chance to move on.

As well as the 'viewpoint' sections in each chapter, we have included a section of questions and answers, which have proved so popular in our previous books. They offer examples of how the strategies and principles we explore might be applied in real-life situations. All the questions are typical ones parents ask on workshops and have been selected for their relevance to each chapter.

CHAPTER 1

A Whole New World

Why this book now? Parenting has changed more in the last 20–30 years than it has for many generations. Of course, society does not stand still, and so each generation faces new challenges when preparing the next generation for the years ahead. But of late, largely due to changes in technology, life has moved so quickly that the life of a young person today will bear little similarity to the lives of his or her grandparents and will yield only some areas of overlap with their parents. What is acceptable in society has changed, how people live and work has changed, and how we relate to the world around us has changed.

In previous generations, marriage and work were seen as life-long choices, whereas now a more flexible attitude to both is common. Even parenting is no longer seen by everyone as the unbreakable bond and unshakeable responsibility of previous generations. Ironically, the number of parents who walk away from their children, and the number of children unable or unwilling to leave their parents, are both growing.

CHANGING TIMES FOR YOUR YOUNG PERSON

There are many reasons why young people stay at home for as long as they do. Some of these are financial: jobs for young people are increasingly hard to come by, and a rate of pay that allows for a standard of living that many consider acceptable may not happen for several years into employment. The dingy, unheated flats that parents may remember might seem unappealing to young people today, many of whom expect at least the same standard of living they enjoyed at home before they will consider a permanent move, even if this means running more than one job to pay for it. This is not true of everyone. For some, the experience of living at home is unbearable, and for any number of reasons as far as these young people are concerned, any independent living, at any standard, is preferable to living at home. It is a shocking indictment on our society that so many young people end up living on the streets in our cities, apparently with no other choices available to them.

There was a time when a young person would leave home because they were unable to do many of the things they wanted while living under their parents' roof. Staying out to all hours, having sex, drinking and socialising were all more difficult to manage at home. Today, most of these problems don't exist. Young people have far greater freedoms, as well as increased privacy to pursue their personal lives, while living at home. For many, moving out and becoming completely independent is as much a financial decision as an emotional or developmental one.

For parents, these changes can be seen in two ways. Many parents are delighted that their child chooses to live in the family home beyond 18 or 21, but by 25 most parents are beginning to wonder when they can expect to get their homes and their lives back. We have met parents of 30-year-olds and beyond who would dearly love their child to move on but feel unable to push them away. This book is designed to help parents deal with the internal and external conflicts of parenting the young adult. How do we prepare them for an independent future? How do we live comfortably together without being too comfortable? How do we allow them the freedom to develop as individuals without compromising our own freedoms and rights? And how do we manage our own changing circumstances and emotional upheavals during this period of change without making them feel responsible or guilty for our insecurities?

The current generation of parents has been more involved in managing their child's life than any previous generation, although, ironically, the result has been that although children today have more freedom they have less independence than in previous years. We strive to let them develop into the person they choose to be, but carefully manage where they go and with whom they spend their time. As a result we are raising a generation of young people who are exceptionally capable and confident in many ways but often lack true socialisation – they do not deal well with others and are inclined to be self-centred and lacking in empathy. They also tend to have very high expectations of life. The all-pervasive media have presented to young people an image of career, relationships and lifestyle that is hedonistic, disposable and, above all, available – and they can be disappointed when it does not appear as anticipated.

Parenting the young adult, then, presents some interesting dilemmas. We want them to be independent, but we need to keep them safe. We want them to be footloose, have fun and to enjoy their youth, but we want them to set firm foundations for the future. We want them to study hard and achieve well, but we want them to be happy. We want them to be independent and free, but we want them to love and need us as much as they always have.

Parenting through this time of change can bring up many personal issues. The concept of the 'empty nest syndrome' is familiar, where parents, particularly mothers, become depressed as their children leave home and feel that their life as they knew it has ended. Tied in with the physical and emotional upheaval of the menopause, this can prove devastating. But fear of these changes can lead parents to hang on to their children or to create dependence in their young people. By unconsciously creating a young person who lacks the confidence or skills to manage alone, a parent can maintain their position within their child's life forever. What we are trying to encourage in this book is a parent who is both willing and able to wave their child off into their future, secure in the knowledge that they have done what they can and that they are ready to begin the new phase of their relationship with their child.

Why we chose the title *Later!*

When we thought about a title for this book we considered many options. Eventually, we settled for the single word 'Later' as an abbreviation of the phrase 'see you later', because that implies leaving – but not for good. There was some discussion across the age ranges about how this should be written. The suggestion 'Laterz' was made, as indeed was 'L8R' but we settled on the more universally readable 'Later' in the hope that it will be more widely understood and prove more lasting.

Later! is the third book in what is intended to be a series of four, looking at parenting in all its changing facets, from the earliest years to supporting a child who is leaving home for good. To most people it would seem logical to have started with the earliest years first and then move through to the oldest, but we have moved in our own mysterious way. Our first book *Whatever!* dealt with teenagers, the second *It's Not Fair!* covered the pre-teen age range of 8 until 12, and this third book covers parenting the 16–23 age group.

This has been a reflection in part of the priorities of Gill's work with parents and schools, and the various issues that have emerged in her workshops. Although Gill's work has traditionally been through schools, since she has branched out into presenting workshops in other venues more and more parents have expressed their concerns, frustrations and insecurities in relation to their older children, many of whom still live at home or have returned after living or studying away. For Alison it has mirrored the process she has been living through with her own family and the discussions she has been having with her four children. For both of us, writing the books has reflected and identified issues we have been living with in our personal and/or professional lives – and we have also learnt much about ourselves.

CASE STUDY: TRUDY, 44

Trudy is a single parent. Her daughter Sarah is 22 and still living at home. Sarah has never had a full-time job and finds work 'boring'. Trudy works as an accounts manager for a national retailer and they share a two-bedroomed flat. Sarah describes her mum as her best friend and they frequently go out together in the evening with Sarah's friends; they will often drink heavily together and go 'partying'.

Sarah's friends are often at the flat and comment on how lucky Sarah is to have such a lovely fun mother.

At home, Sarah spends most of her time online or watching TV. What money she has comes from a small amount of benefit money and supplements from her mother. Her father left some years before and still occasionally provides gifts or cash handouts for Sarah. She speaks to him regularly on the phone but rarely sees him, as he has another family.

Trudy has few friends of her own age. She says that being with people over 40 makes her feel old, and she prefers the company of Sarah and her friends. She would like Sarah to take more responsibility in the home, to clean and tidy, to shop and prepare food or at least to take care of her own laundry and ironing. Presently, Trudy is responsible for all the household tasks, although Sarah will sometimes help if specifically asked to.

Sarah has no real qualifications and no ambitions. She expects that she will eventually find somebody with money to marry her and will be kept by her husband. She would like to have children one day but wants to employ a nanny to do the work and does not expect to have to care for herself in any way. She describes herself as 'lazy'.

Trudy wishes that Sarah would 'grow up' and sometimes despairs for her future. She sometimes feels sorry for herself that she has such a helpless and selfish daughter, although she loves her.

The co-dependent relationship

We have chosen this case study as an example of the co-dependent relationship that sometimes exists between a parent and a child. Thankfully, most relationships are not as damaged or damaging as this example, but there are some elements here that may be reflected in more functional families. Trudy is not taking responsibility for her daughter's lack of maturity and development. She is blaming Sarah for it, but it is clear that Trudy is not herself fully mature, as she is still clinging to the life of a 22-year-old and has allowed her daughter to carry on being a child too. Most parents would have put their foot down a long time ago, even if it meant being unpopular. But as Trudy is unwilling to grow up herself, it's perhaps unreasonable to expect her daughter to do so without any support.

The difficulty now is that Trudy has a lot to lose if she becomes unpopular with her daughter. She stands to lose her social life and her role as a 'lovely mum'. She wants change but only without risking the present state of the relationship – and that has resulted in her difficult position.

This brings us to an important point: how do we support our

children to go beyond our limitations, and to be bigger and better people than us if that is what they choose to be, without those very differences seeming like criticisms or failings in ourselves? Is it possible to teach someone to be something we are not, to do things of which we are not capable?

How do we react to our children?

Looking into the face of your young adult can feel like looking into a mirror at a person who is both like and unlike you. Although we can often see their failings better than we can see our own, we can also see their strengths too. Most parents at some stage will have felt a pang of envy at the fresh-faced enthusiasm and potential of youth, and while for many this is a source of pride, there are some parents who unwittingly allow their feelings of inadequacy or envy to become damaging. Most of the time the experience of living with parents is familiar – there are good times and bad times, rows, laughter, fun, stress and frustrations – a whole range of family experiences. The jealous parent only shows their true colours when their child gets the opportunity to do something special or to shine. Most parents are delighted and excited for their child; a few, however, will make some comment or criticism to dampen the mood. There is a difficult path to tread between injecting a note of realism and actively discouraging, through being overly critical or consistently finding a way to belittle achievements and dampen enthusiasms. For many of these parents their behaviour is almost automatic, they don't mean to be negative but rather relaying the 'don't get your hopes up' and 'nobody likes someone who blows their own trumpet' attitudes they were raised with becomes second nature. The behaviour seems to happen more commonly within same-sex relationships, so mother to daughter, or father to son – perhaps because the mirror image is closer to the original or the competition within the family that is well observed in animal behaviour is taking place here too.

Anyone watching *The X Factor* auditions on TV will have been struck by the attitudes of family to the aspiring competitors. Most are excited and nervous for their child, a few will be preparing them for failure and some are blindly encouraging, regardless of talent. One can only assume these same characteristics are carried through in other areas of the family life. Some of us firmly believe in visualising success, others think that if you expect the worst you will only ever have nice surprises – and the balance just believe in getting on with it. Interestingly, everyone believes they face reality!

Most of us fall into one of three categories as a parent:

1 **The blind enthusiast** This is the parent who believes their child to be fabulous (as of course they are) and will not accept anyone's criticism, however well meant or helpful. This parent believes the way to help their child succeed is to encourage them to understand that everything they do is right and every failure is down to someone else. This is the kind of parent most parents wish they had had! 'Don't listen to them darling, they're just jealous!'

2 **The realist** This parent tends to avoid extremes of praise or criticism. They let their head rule their heart. They listen, they think and then they say and do what will be most helpful and useful in a given situation. They try to encourage everyone else to consider and celebrate, plan and reflect unemotionally. 'That sounds an interesting plan; tell me about what you might do if things turn out differently.'

3 **The critic** This parent believes that the only way to get better at anything is to overcome failings, and the only way to overcome failings is to know what they are. They believe it is a part (and sometimes a painful part) of their job as a parent to point out such failings or perceived potential pitfalls in any plan. 'But just

looking at it from Ellie's point of view rather than yours, it looks pretty selfish to me.'

The changing face of parenting

The truth is that parenting is a minute-by-minute role. Just when you think it's going well, something can happen to send it all topsy-turvy again, and when life seems dire, a moment of intimacy and joy can spring from nowhere. A good parent is sometimes the blind enthusiast, sometimes the realist and sometimes the critic. The trick is knowing when to be which. By and large, a realistic approach is the one that enables a young person to make their own decisions and take responsibility for the outcomes, but there are times when having someone steadfastly in your corner is what is needed – and others when tough love is what is needed.

EXERCISE: Reflection (just for fun!) – what kind of parent are you?

Ring the answer A, B or C that is most typical of your immediate response. It may well be that you will at some time use all three approaches. If this is the case, ring the one that you would use first.

Question 1

Your child comes home from college/university very excited that they have been short-listed for a grant-bearing award with 99 other young people. If successful, they will be given a substantial amount of money to travel for a month in South America with five other young people from around the country.

Do you?

A Ask lots of questions to find out the details and wish them luck.

B Jump about excitedly, high-fiving them.

C Point out to them how many other people are in the running for this award and how low the odds of success are? Also mention the potential dangers of such a trip that might make being unsuccessful a good result.

Question 2

Your young adult is heartbroken. Their boyfriend/girlfriend of one month has broken off the relationship. They adored this partner and lavished affection and attention on them. They believed the partner felt the same way.

Do you?

A Listen, if need be, over and over again. Sympathise with their hurt and, when they are ready, help them identify ways of getting over it.

B Call the ex- every name under the sun. Tell your child that they are wonderful and don't deserve to be treated that way. Threaten to go round and give him/her a piece of your mind.

C Let them know that there are plenty more fish in the sea and that wearing your heart on your sleeve is a sure recipe for getting hurt. Suggest that maybe next time they should play it a little more distantly if they don't want to scare the other person off.

Question 3

A frequently grumpy and unfriendly neighbour has complained about music being played at high volume in your home and suggests it is happening when you are out.

Do you?

A Discuss with the whole family acceptable levels of noise at different times of the day, for different equipment in the home; for example, the television in the bedroom turned to level 6 volume after 10.00 pm and level 3 after midnight.

B Tell the neighbour to get lost (or worse) and point out that your family is entitled to do as it pleases in your own home as long as each person is responsible – and that as far as you're concerned, they are always responsible.

C Tell your young adult off for upsetting the neighbour, because it's you that has to take the criticism. Point out that they are being selfish and unfair to you and the neighbour. Tell them they are breaking your trust by behaving this way when you are not around.

Question 4

Your young adult cooks a meal for the family from scratch for the first time. The menu is a little over-ambitious and much of the food is cold or undercooked, but he or she has tried to create something spectacular. They are a little upset that the end result is not as good as they had intended.

Do you?

A Tell them how proud you are of them. Praise the ambition and creativity of the meal. Tell them all the things you enjoyed and encourage other family members to do the same. Help them identify how they can avoid the pitfalls next time.

B Tell them it is the best meal you have ever tasted. Eat everything on the table with relish and delight regardless. When they express disappointment, tell them they are wrong and that everything is wonderful.

C Go through everything they have done in detail pointing out what they have done well and how they could improve the things they have done not so well. Talk to them about timing and how to plan a meal so that everything is ready at the same time.

Question 5

Your young person has left the house in a hurry. Their breakfast dishes are unwashed, the kitchen is in a state and there is a trail of towels, clothes, magazines, books and papers all over the place. You have to leave for work yourself.

Do you?

A Send them a text message asking them to ensure they have tidied up by the time you and the family get home even if that means changing their plans.

B Feel a bit annoyed but, after all, you're only young once. Do a quick pick-up and tidy, and resolve to do the rest when you get home.

C Tidy it yourself after work, feeling resentful, and when they eventually get home point out how selfish they are, how busy you are and how it is unfair that you should have to pick up after them now that they are grown up.

Question 6

Your 17-year-old son asks if he can have a party for his eighteenth birthday. He is only going to invite 15 friends, but he would like you to go out for the evening.

Do you?

A Discuss as a whole family how this might be managed. Get your son to draw up a realistic budget, to think about what he needs to do to prepare the house: does anything need to be put away, how many people do you need to do the shifting, and who is going to do the work. Talk to him about security and what he will do if things get out of hand in any way. Encourage him to think about what else needs to be done, such as warning the neighbours, ensuring those he invites do not make the party information more widely available, making a clear smoking area, protecting valuables and pets, and so on.

B Be delighted that your young person has decided to celebrate their birthday at home, as it shows just how much the family means to them. Decide that because you trust them, and you have made this clear to them, to take this opportunity for a weekend away yourself.

C Refuse point blank.

What kind of parent or you?

Mostly As You are inclined to be a realistic parent. You are encouraging, kind and thoughtful but you also see the problems when they arise. You help your child to sort out their own problems rather than doing them for them, and you put their needs before your desire for popularity or approval.

POSITIVES You are someone they can trust and will come to with problems, because they know you will not judge.

NEGATIVES They will not always see you as 'fun' and may construe your consistency as predictability. They may find you a bit boring.

Mostly Bs You are inclined to be blindly enthusiastic. You are staunchly on your child's side, no matter what. There is nothing they can do or say in the world that you will not back up. The only person who you feel has the right to criticise them is yourself – and you do it rarely. You encourage them in everything they do and back them up to the hilt.

POSITIVES You are the parent everybody thinks they want. You are endlessly supportive and encouraging, and can always be relied on to come up trumps in a problem. Your child can always depend on you to be there for them.

NEGATIVES Your child may never truly grow up, because they never have to take responsibility for anything. There is a difference between self-esteem and self-delusion and the offspring of blindly enthusiastic parents may have an unrealistic and over-inflated sense of their own abilities and worth in relation to others. They may lack empathy and care for others, be unable to take any criticism and resist authority or rules.

Mostly Cs You are inclined to be a critical parent. You often point out the (sometimes obvious) failings of others, because you believe they need to be aware of this in order to improve. Your motivations are to help your young adult to be better than they are – but you may be inclined to nag a little.

POSITIVES Having boundaries is a good thing, and children and young people do best in an atmosphere where boundaries are clear and well established. You believe in boundaries and maintain them even when it's hard to do so. You encourage your child to think of others and the greater good in everything they do and to see the bigger picture rather than getting hung up in the details and emotions of life.

NEGATIVES If you are very critical, they may feel they can never do anything right. You might also find that they are inclined to lie or withhold from you as a way of avoiding your criticism. They are unlikely to share problems or details of their life with you if they feel that you will always pick out their failings. If you are inclined to nag they will simply stop listening to you and will have learnt to tune you out by the time they had reached adolescence.

What is the ideal parent?

The ideal parent is mostly realistic, but occasionally blindly enthusiastic and, when necessary, critical. Given that all three types of parent tend to think they are being realistic, this book will explore the overlaps – and the realities – from the points of view of both parent and young person.

Parents often want to know how they can tell if they are doing a good job. The simple answer is that a child who is doing well is evidence of a parent doing their job well. We believe that a child doing well is one who is succeeding on their own terms, in their chosen areas regardless of any limiting factors. Having a brilliant well-paid career but feeling alienated from their own children or partner is not truly successful. On the other hand, managing a loving home, maintaining a good relationship, raising happy, healthy children – if that is a choice they make – and finding a way of contributing to the world can be counted as successful. Whether a child becomes a media mogul, a shelf stacker in a supermarket, a high-flying surgeon, a pipe fitter or runs a small online business is not important. What matters is that they have reached their potential, continue to create opportunities for themselves to increase their personal development, and that they have a meaningful and loving life where they give and receive care and intimacy. How, what and where this is done are infinitely variable, but the outcomes are not.

CASE STUDY: DANIEL, 22

Daniel is the middle child of three and his older brother, Michael, currently works in the US as a rising star in a large multinational corporation. His younger sister, Emily, is at university studying law. His mother, Carla, has a successful interior design company and his father, David, runs a computer software company.

Daniel was late developing speech and struggled at primary school. He was un-coordinated and found reading and writing difficult – eventually being identified as dyslexic when he was seven as well as having other learning difficulties. He was a popular and kind child, but his confidence was not good, due to his problems. His older brother was a star student who went to the same school, and Daniel suffered from the expectations of others based on his brother.

He left school at 16 and found part-time work as an office cleaner, which he did for two years before attending the local college full time for a year to study for GCSEs. He successfully gained six A–C GCSEs and found work in a large sports shop.

Both his parents have supported him unconditionally and spent a lot of time helping him overcome his poor self-esteem. His girlfriend moved into his family home when he was 18, as she was desperate to leave hers. They have been together since he was 17. She works on the beauty counter at a local department store.

Daniel has been promoted at work to a section management role and is now studying maths A-level at college supported by his work. He moved out of home when he was 20 and bought a one-bedroomed flat with his girlfriend through a shared ownership scheme run by a local housing association. His parents are openly proud of him and all he has achieved, and they maintain a close relationship, frequently at each other's homes and going out together for meals or social events.

He has a close relationship with his sister, who phones and visits frequently, although not with his brother. Both parents express concern that Michael is not doing as well as Daniel.

Daniel's parents love all their children equally, as most parents do, but they managed to bring them up as individuals with different needs and skills in such a way that they could strive for success on their own terms – not in competition with each other.

So often a bright or high-achieving sibling can lead to brothers and sisters who feel second best or in their sibling's shadow. Not so with Daniel. He learnt that he could be successful by working hard, just as his brother and sister had done, but he also learnt that we can set our own goals – and achieving them feels good, whatever they are.

Perhaps Michael still has to learn to allow himself to reach goals. He is still trying to meet the standards set by others in a very competitive field without reflecting on personal happiness or satisfaction. For him, the goal posts move every time he gets close. He has made status, money and prestige his aims – and they are notoriously hard to satisfy. Almost no one who makes money their marker of success will ever have enough.

CHANGING TIMES FOR YOU

Although we consider the changing times we live in, and the changing times for our children and families as they become adults, we also need to consider the changing times for ourselves as parents whose role is moving away from being one that is central to our lives and everything we do. Emotionally, we never stop being a parent, but in our day-to-day lives our role as a parent becomes less and less central.

It is important to consider ourselves as individuals throughout these changing times to reconnect to what we want, how we live our lives and what is important to us. The changing role of parents can feel like something has been lost or outgrown, but it can also feel like a new era of change and excitement, of possibility and freedom. For most people it is probably a bit of both.

How we respond to the changes in our role will depend on many factors. The greatest influence will probably be how we view life and change in general. We have already explored three characteristics of a parent: the blind enthusiast, the realist and the critic. We are likely to bring these same qualities into play when embarking on a new adventure. Some of us will weigh up the pros and cons of the situation, will set goals and will make plans. Others will be signing up for online dating, booking a cruise, buying a whole new wardrobe or converting the newly vacated room into a gym. And others will dwell on all that will be hard or difficult or sad – all the negatives. For some, change is exciting, for some a challenge and for others change is frightening. How we choose to deal with it will depend on the emotions we attach to it in the first place. If we view it as an opportunity, a new phase and something exciting to do, we are more likely to bring enthusiasm and creativity to bear on the choices we make. If we approach it with dread and fear, or see it as a time of loss, we are more likely to use avoidance techniques, addictions (acknowledged or denied), apply comfort behaviours and experience depression.

How we approach change will also determine how we behave with our young adults. If we embrace change, we are more likely to encourage them to be independent, because we will manage and take responsibility for our own feelings rather than letting our fears stand in the way of their future. They will also learn by imitation that change is exciting, powerful and provides endless opportunities. If we resist change we may, albeit unconsciously, encourage them to stay children for longer – to maintain both their role as dependant and ours as carer. We may also teach them to fear change and to avoid decision-making and risk, preferring to stay safe and unchallenged.

A reality check

If you completed the reflection task on pages 9–13, you will have identified for yourself what kind of parent you are. This may also give you a clue about how you are with yourself too. If you are sufficiently brave, why not give the questions and answers to your young adult and ask them to complete them about you? Ask them to identify which of the answers they think most suits you and your style of parenting. Did they think of you in the same way as you did yourself? What does this tell you?

Maybe this experience has delivered some reinforcement of your self-view, but possibly you have also been given some surprising information. Consider this as an opportunity to grow. In the middle of a busy family, there can be insufficient time to think about who we are. Time alone is rare – and so often taken up with maintenance of one kind or another. But as time passes you will, if you choose, have more time to think about you: who you are; what you want; your hopes, dreams and aspirations. You may choose to pick up on some that you had when you were younger, or you may decide to re-examine how you live now and make some changes, big or small, to support your own well-being and the next period of your life.

EXERCISE: Approaching change

Here are some simple questions to help you consider your attitude to change. Write down the answer that pops into your head first – try not to 'over-think' your answer.

1 Q: How did you feel on your first day at secondary school?

   A:

2 Q: How did you feel the first time you walked into your first independent home?

   A:

3 Q: How did you feel the first time you went on holiday without your parents?

   A:

4 Q: When was the first time you remember feeling grown up?

   A:

5 Q: How far and for how long would you feel comfortable travelling alone?

   A:

6 Q: How many different jobs have you had?

   A:

7 Q: Have you ever stayed in a job where you were unhappy? For how long?

   A:

8 Q: What colours are you wearing today and what colours did you wear yesterday?

   A:

9 Q: Have you ever stayed in a relationship where you were unhappy? For how long?

   A:

10 Q: Which things do you do on set days of the week (for example, laundry on Wednesday or shopping on Saturday)?

   A:

The first three questions are about doing new things by yourself. Most people will have written 'excitement' or 'fear'. Some people will have written both, and others will have found a way of including both. Some people will have found other words such as 'anxious' or 'free' or 'grown-up' to express how they felt. Only you can decide whether the feelings you have written down relate more to excitement or fear. Someone who embraces change well will probably have a mixture of excitement and fear at the same time; they are two sides of the same coin. The difference between the two is in the expectation – the appreciation of what happens next. Fear is when the *negative* possibilities seem very real, and excitement when the *positives* seem very real. If your answers show a balance, you are probably neither a risk-taker nor are you inhibited when it comes to making changes. If your answers showed more fear or anxiety, perhaps you have a slightly pessimistic view of change, and if all your answers show excitement, perhaps you are more inclined to take risks.

Question 4 is all about self-reflection. There have probably been many times in your life when you have felt grown up, but which one did you choose? Was it the first time you tied your shoe laces for yourself? Or the first time you went to school by yourself? Or the first time you held your new child in your arms? All of these things probably felt grown up at the time, but are you filtering your memories through an older and wiser head? If you are being selective and can see that there were previous times when you felt grown up but you have dismissed them, perhaps you are someone who doesn't give yourself enough credit for the small changes and choices in life.

Question 5 speaks for itself. How much confidence do you have in yourself and your own ability to take care of yourself and to meet your own needs? Is your identity bound up in other people, or do you have the confidence that wherever you go you will meet people you can relate to and with whom you can form relationships? How big a factor in your response is fear?

Questions 6 and 7 are about different ways in which we create change in our lives. If you have had many different jobs (even with the same employer), you are probably someone who is stimulated by change. If you have not, you are probably someone for whom the fear of change is a barrier. You probably feel that what is known and safe is preferable to what is unknown and unpredictable, although obviously choices are influenced by the availability of resources and our relationship with others – this can give us a 'let out' for doing nothing.

Question 8. The colours we wear may also be an indicator of adaptability and change. Some people match their mood to their colours, others prefer to stay with the same palette. Which are you? Do you let everyone know how you're feeling or do you prefer to be or seem consistent?

Questions 7 and 9 give an indication of how great the influence of fear is in your personal or professional life. For some people, the fear of change is greater than dealing with unhappiness. Even unhappiness can provide a kind of security: we may not like it, but we know what to expect. Ending a relationship or changing a job can feel so risky that for some people staying with what is known is preferable. It's interesting that some people will leave a relationship but stay in a job where they feel unhappy – and vice versa. Others will stay in both, or choose to leave.

We all have different areas of confidence within us. Some of us are confident at work, some in our personal lives. It can be hard to believe that someone who is dynamic and go-getting professionally would put up with an unhappy relationship, but it happens all the time. How much would you be prepared to put up with in order to maintain the status quo?

Question 10 is about routine and habit. We all have routines and patterns in our lives, and they often make life easier. When we are following a pattern, we don't have to think about it very much, so we avoid the need to make constant decisions. Sometimes, however, patterns run us. For some people, everything in their life is a routine and they feel unable to break or change them. This can get to harmful levels if individuals feel imprisoned by irrational routines such as obsessive hand washing, which can take over their lives. And for us all there are times when routines instead of supporting our life make it harder. Have you ever told yourself, 'I have to ...' when actually you didn't have to at all?

Embracing change

Whether we like it or not, change happens. We cannot prevent the world around us, and the people in our lives, from changing, moving and sometimes leaving. People we love and who love us sometimes move away, sometimes leave home and sometimes leave us altogether, because they move into new circles, new places, or perhaps even die.

It is easy to feel that every change is an ending of something. That which was is now no longer. It is also possible to see each change as a potential new beginning. Every good thing in your life had a beginning, and every one of those beginnings came with a change. Everything you love started somewhere – and that somewhere was a change. The difference is about perspective. When we look backwards, it's easy to see new beginnings; and if we look forward and anticipate losses, it's because the new things have not yet begun.

It is not easy, and perhaps not possible, for everyone to see change as potential for good, but remembering positive changes that have occurred helps us to keep perspective. Take time to reflect on all the good and positive things in your life and where they came from, the moment they arrived and the opportunity that allowed the arrival to take place; for example, Alison and Gill often reflect on how they met and began writing together. They were both living independent lives, and then circumstances brought them together. Alison attended a workshop run by Gill. She saw a potential for change and took a risk by asking Gill to collaborate on a book. Gill saw a potential change and took a risk by deciding to do something different and work with Alison. The rest is history. But along the way there were many opportunities where fear of rejection, fear of not being good enough, or simply fear of change could have stopped them.

One of the things people do when facing their fears is to keep busy. It stops the fear from taking over. Unfortunately, this can also stop us being able to reflect positively and embrace the excitement of change too. Fear cannot hurt us, it's just a feeling, so giving ourselves time to explore the fear – and the associated excitement – is important. Whether it's a long bath, a walk with the dog, a couple of hours with a cup of coffee or a chat to a friend or counsellor, it doesn't matter. What matters is that we allow the process to happen. And although we might not be in control we

can make sure that we are not overwhelmed by allowing ourselves
time to reflect on the process of change around us and the impact
it is having on us.

QUESTIONS AND ANSWERS

Q: 'I have told my son he has to do his ironing. He won't, so I end
up doing it because I don't want him going out looking scruffy or
people thinking we are a family that doesn't have standards. How
do I get him to do his own ironing?'

A: From what you have said, it sounds as if your reason for wanting to have him wear ironed clothes is not about him but rather
about you, and your concern for what people will think. If you
really want him to take responsibility for his own ironing (or
anything else) then you have to be prepared to hand over the
responsibility for it to him – and his options include deciding
not to bother. Make sure you have taught him to do it properly –
the assumption that anyone can iron is not true, and it's harder
than it looks. Try holding up an ironed shirt and an unironed
one next to each other and asking him if he can see the difference. But from then on, it's up to him. Why would anyone do a
task that is difficult or that he does not enjoy if someone else is
willing to do it for him?

Q: 'My daughter has never left home. Now 25, she started three
different university courses, completing none of them, and has
remained based in her room at home. She has a really comfortable
life, a good job and is able to spend her income on going out and
enjoying herself, safe in the knowledge that there is a life here to
support and provide for her everyday needs. But we want her to
be independent and make her own choices – how can we encourage her to move on with her life?'

A: By removing the security blanket. Start by asking that she pays
a reasonable amount into the family kitty and stop providing

meals at convenient times. Discuss with her that if she does want to stay at home, life henceforth would work better as a flat-share model, with her doing her own shopping, cooking and cleaning, and while you are happy to see her, it is time she moved on. It may be that she feels insecure about trying to establish life on her own – and perhaps you could talk to her frankly about this – but it may also be that she simply lacks the motivation, because life at home is just too comfortable.

CHAPTER 2

Grow up! How to Encourage the Development of Appropriate Life Skills

What constitutes a life skill varies according to whom you ask. To a teacher, relevant life skills will mean things like being able to take part in discussions, problem solving, making choices, recognising and dealing with difficult emotions and managing relationships of all kinds.

Ask a parent, however, and the list is long, varied and all-encompassing. Although the issues isolated already would be included, the list would probably also feature a range of personal management skills, such as arranging for regular check-ups with the dentist and remembering to buy deodorant. A life skill is essentially anything we do that enables us to live our lives and, like all skills, it requires both a degree of knowledge (why should clothes be properly clean rather than just look clean?) as well as a range of attitudes and values without which many of the skills would be pointless ('I am worth taking care of', 'treating others with respect matters').

LIFE SKILLS FOR YOUR
YOUNG PERSON

When we are trying to teach or develop life skills with young people there are times when we need to explain and provide knowledge; at other times we need to place those skills within a framework of attitudes and values. Skills also need practice. Understanding why we do them is important, but it does not make us better at them; for example, we can learn all about nutrition and cooking techniques, we can understand the importance of food to well-being and nurture, but all this understanding won't make us a good cook. Only hands-on experience will ultimately change our ability to make a meal. Practice alone does not ensure success. Some people have a creative flair with food whereas some try hard but never get there; without practice, success is unlikely.

What are the life skills young people need?

Life skills are both the most basic and the most frequently used skills that a young person needs if they are to function as an independent adult. These will include essential skills – cooking, cleaning, laundry, personal hygiene – as well as how to manage several aspects of life at the same time, such as getting to work or lectures on time, but also having enough to eat and finding a way to get home.

Individual life skills – mundane tasks such as ironing, washing-up, cleaning the bath, changing the duvet, laundry in all its complexities, changing a light bulb, sewing on a button or mending a hem – can be learnt quite easily. Some people learn these in childhood or adolescence as part of a family, through the tasks that family members undertake for themselves and each other.

As they get older they need to learn more complex skills and to synchronise them, so basic study skills become a much more complicated time-management issue where many aspects of life need to be skilfully juggled. Shopping needs to be bought in order that food can be made, a (reasonably) balanced diet needs to be eaten in order to function correctly, sleep needs to be taken in order to be able to learn, studying needs to be completed in the context of enjoying a social life. And into this complex mixture come the needs to manage money (and possibly to earn it as well) and to maintain good relationships with friends and family. And through this wider consideration, the complicated basis on which our adult lives are grounded (or perhaps not) becomes more apparent.

True independence comes when an individual is able to manage all these issues for themselves. If you can secure a high-powered job, but you can't boil an egg, you are still dependent on others. In modern society we all rely on a variety of external services and skills – but the life skills of an individual are those that enable them to live healthily and soundly without recourse to others. A person might choose to hire someone to clean for them, but they still need to be able to understand the processes, both in order to make up short-term deficiencies and to effectively explain and evaluate what is being done for them. A person might choose to hire someone to care for their children for some part of the day, but they will also need to understand how it is done when they are on their own or when additional support is not there.

Developing life skills with your young adult

The purpose of supporting the development of life skills for your young adult is to see them off into their future as independent young people who are capable of managing all aspects of their physical and emotional well-being. This doesn't mean they will; it just means that they can.

Gill recently met a mother of two who described herself as the most laid-back mother on the planet and who airily announced that she hadn't taught her kids anything. She left them free to enjoy their youth by absorbing all responsibility for their chores and life management. She had decided that whatever they needed to learn at a later date, they would. We rather suspect that it is more likely that these two will have unrealistic views of what living and managing themselves entail and will be inclined to expect a great deal from those around them. We don't just learn how to manage the chores when we learn to be independent, we also learn about what others do for us and why, about interdependence and community, about empathy and duty.

We have arranged our list of skills into two parts: the practical skills, and the social and emotional skills. Each of these two parts also has two levels of complexity, the first is a straightforward skill-development list, the second involves a level of choice and decision-making.

EXERCISE: Reflection – practical skills

To help you identify the skills to work on with your young people, here is a list of practical skills. Firstly, ask yourself how important you consider the skill to be in the life of an independent young person, and we suggest you grade each skill from 1 to 3, from very important to not important at all. Secondly, ask yourself whether, to the best of your knowledge, your child has ever completed this task unaided. Award a tick, cross or question mark as appropriate.

	Importance?	Completed?
Cooking a meal for a family or group of friends		
Completing a week's wash		
Booking an appointment at a doctor's surgery and filling in a prescription		
Booking a check-up at a dentist		
Planning a complex journey		
Managing a weekly shop on a budget		
Changing a bed		
Putting a plug on something		
Cleaning a room effectively and understanding the best order in which to do this		
Laying a table		
Sewing on a button		
Repairing an item of clothing (torn jeans perhaps)		
Sorting and putting out the rubbish and recycling		
Packing a bag for several days away		

Once you have worked through the list, perhaps your young person could also have a go? Ask them to look through the list and see whether their answers are different from yours. Do they rank the same activities as important? Do they feel they have completed the same things that you have identified? This may provide you with an opportunity to talk about why these things matter and to encourage them to develop their own skills in preparation for independent living.

If they are shortly to leave home, you could use the list above as a checklist for developing and practising the skills in the available time. Use the 'importance' column to prioritise and to tick off the skills once they have been practised.

The next level of skills is still practical, but these involve a degree of choice. Making choices is a skill in its own right and one that can take a lifetime to truly develop. For most of us there are times when we don't want to have to make any more decisions – usually when we've made a few bad ones. Perhaps our choice-making abilities need a rest, just like our muscles!

	Importance?	Completed?
Researching where to go for hair-dressing/cutting and booking an appointment		
Researching phone contracts and deciding on the best deal for their own needs and usage pattern		
Booking a journey involving changes of transport; finding the cheapest and quickest routes		
Planning a meal, shopping for it and cooking it for a group of people		
Organising and arranging an outing or event for a group of people coming from different places		
Reviewing a current utility supplier and comparing with competitors to see if it is the best choice		
Researching and organising a family day out within a budget		

The purpose of these more complex tasks is not only to practise the tasks themselves but also to see how they work in combination. Their completion will also help a young adult to see what's involved and to be able to juggle different priorities against needs, wants and limitations – in other words, practising skills used in everyday life.

It's an interesting point that younger children (aged 10 or 11 years) would often love to do these kinds of tasks but are seldom allowed to. By the time they are 17 or 18 they may be less enthusiastic, unless they can see an end result for themselves. Helping them to see the payback in terms of financial gain, satisfaction of self and others and the feel-good factor will help encourage them to involve themselves.

How do you get them to learn practical life skills – especially if they don't want to?

The answer is simple: stop doing it for them. Necessity is not only the mother of invention but it is also the mother of personal development. By withdrawing your willingness to support them in these tasks they will have to do them for themselves – but don't be surprised if they choose to go without. I'm thinking in particular of ironing. Many young people do not do their own ironing, and if parent labour is withdrawn, they still won't do their own ironing. This leaves a parent with a choice: either they do it for them or they let them go out looking creased. Some parents we have spoken with find it impossible to allow their young adult to be seen in public all crumpled; probably because they feel it reflects badly on them as a parent. Personally, we believe that if we remove the consequence from a choice, we take away the need for a choice. If one or other parent is going to carry on doing the ironing, even if their child says no, why on earth would that child ever say yes? Very few people love ironing.

Not only are there choices that need to be made on an individual level but there are also responsibilities that come with being part of a family. These responsibilities grow with age and independence just as freedoms do. A young person who wants to be treated as an equal adult needs to take responsibility within the family as an equal adult too. This needs to be clearly stated and backed up in practice. A young adult living at home who refuses to do their share of the cleaning, even when asked, cannot expect to be allowed favours such as a lift into town or the use of the car in return.

They may need careful guidance to understand what is required; what is obvious to us may not be so to them. We may need to itemise the chores and responsibilities they are expected to complete. In a busy home this can seem very natural, as all members of the family may have their own chore list or rota, but in a smaller or quieter family it may seem quite artificial, and may be best handled through a discussion at a family meeting rather than a list on the wall.

As your young adult grows older they will be moving more towards the role of lodger within the home as you take less and less responsibility for them; have less access to their life and less influence over their choices. This will involve moving to an understanding that you are sharing a space together as equals; you are not responsible for them and their welfare, they are.

Although they will never be completely independent in your home, you should be aiming for them to be as independent as possible so that they can move on when the time is right, with the core skills in place to live successfully without you.

CASE STUDY: LAURA, 19

Laura went away to university in London having been raised in a small town near Sunderland. She went into a shared house with three other young women of a similar age and a 24-year-old man.

The first week was busy and exciting, and the group spent a lot of time together because they didn't know anyone else. During this week it became apparent that between them they had very limited skills. Laura was the only one who could work a washing machine and knew how to sort laundry to prevent colours running. None of them had ever changed a duvet before and two of the girls and the man had no idea how to prepare a simple meal without a microwave.

After three months, the house was in a very shabby state,

as no one understood or recognised the need for proper cleaning. They had organised a rota for shopping, cooking, washing-up and vacuuming, which was generally adhered to, but they had created a new clause that meant if the shopping person had forgotten to shop, or if the cooking person wasn't in the mood, then that person could buy chips for all instead. This meant the washing-up person was off the hook too and everyone was meant to take care of their own cups and dishes. The vacuuming person was allowed to renege on their task if the others did the same, in the interests of fairness.

Eventually, they were living on chips, the kitchen was piled high with unwashed dishes, the floor and carpets were littered and dirty and the fridge was empty. Relationships within the group began to break down quite seriously with factions forming. Everyone blamed each other for the state of the house and no one took responsibility for organising and implementing change. Eventually, Laura moved out and into a shared flat with two young women who were well organised and motivated to keep their home liveable and comfortable and to take care of themselves effectively.

EXERCISE: Reflection – emotional and social skills

It is far easier to create a checklist for practical skills than it is for emotional and social skills. Generally, it is pretty easy to say whether someone can sew on a button or not, although it could be argued that there are still levels of performance even for such a clear task. Perhaps we should say sewing on a button that will still be there in three months' time!

With regard to emotional and social skills, it is not so much a case of whether they have these skills as whether they use them effectively. And if so, do they use them all the time or just when they think about it? We are not asking you to identify how important you think these elements are – we have already suggested these as the areas of emotional and social well-being that support the individual and the wider groups they may find themselves in. We are asking you this time simply to think about your young adult and to gauge honestly the level of their skills development. We have written the desired end result, so the question is: how often does your young person achieve this end result? To be clear, we are not asking you to say if they are *capable* of it (we think all young adults are capable of achieving these things), what we are asking is *how often do they achieve them* – often, sometimes or never?

Complete the following tick chart for your young adult. You may like to share your results with them as a way of helping them reflect on their behaviour and skills development.

	Often or always	Sometimes	Almost never
Negotiating a fair solution to a problem or conflict that all can live with, such as what to watch on television			
Managing money			
Dealing with strong feelings appropriately			
Expressing anger over something and being able to progress without hanging on to it			
Being able to make themselves heard			
Negotiating through problems			
Balancing the social side of life with other things			
Managing commitments and being someone others find reliable			
Having integrity – being someone others believe in; having a good reputation			
Being able to empathise and see the other person's point of view			

	Often or always	Sometimes	Almost never
Letting go of what is not important and choosing your battles			
Compromising			
Neighbourhood cooperation and awareness of others, noise and freedom versus the preferences of others			

Developing emotional and social skills

Many people feel that these skills come with age. This is simply not true. We do develop further as we grow older simply because the opportunities to practise are greater, but there are many people who never learn to manage anger effectively or to negotiate a fair solution, choosing instead to always try to win. The world is full of people who cannot manage strong feelings without a glass in one hand or a cigarette in the other – or worse. These skills are among the most important things a person can learn, but just like the practical skills it is possible to manage in life without them. An individual may not feel any great loss or disadvantage from the lack of these skills, but society at large and the people around them will suffer. More and more we are seeing the impact of young people raised to think only of themselves and the impact this will have on the wider society should concern us all.

Helping young people to develop emotional and social skills is helping them to be likeable. Popular young people usually get on well with others of all ages and in all settings, not just their friends.

If you can see that your young adult has room for improvement with their social and emotional skills, encourage them to reflect on how they react and behave in certain settings rather than telling them that they are in some way inadequate, lacking or unskilled. The ability to reflect is also a social and emotional skill and is linked strongly to self-esteem. Reflecting on one's short-comings may be helpful, but only if one has the maturity and self-worth to do so honestly in the first place and without blame or self-recrimination in the second. The ideal situation is for a young person to recognise that there are some things they need to work on and to be able to talk through possible changes that they might make.

CASE STUDY: STEPHEN, 18

Stephen has a terrible temper and has had his family tiptoeing around him for years. He had trouble at school too and his family are worried about what will happen when he takes up his university place later in the year. He is not usually violent, but he regularly becomes verbally aggressive, saying cruel and hurtful things, and in the past this has ended friendships and relationships.

The first step was for his family to let him know how it felt to be on the receiving end of his anger and the impact he had had on the family over the years. This was handled sensitively and with concern for his future, not with blame for the past. The whole family sat together and discussed the future, including changes to the washing-up rota, the bedroom allocation and how they felt about him not being at home during term times. They then eased lovingly into their concern, and Stephen admitted he also had worries about his temper and its effects on his future friendships and working relationships. His parents asked him to identify what the triggers for these rages have been – the moment where he felt himself lose control. Once he had identified the triggers (sometimes a look, or someone laughing at him, or feeling that the other person wasn't listening, or feeling criticised, and so on) he was able to identify a better course of action than shouting and screaming. This was sometimes by making a comment, walking away or taking a moment to let the feelings settle, and sometimes just letting the person know how angry their action was making him feel. Stephen and his parents were well aware that just coming up with an alternative action would not change a habitual response easily or without practice. People experience anger in a very different part of the brain from rational thought, and bringing one to bear on the other takes both intention and practice.

Stephen appreciated the concern and the support, and began to work on changing his responses to triggers. When he tried to do it differently, his parents helped him to reflect on how it went and how it felt, and this was managed both with recognition of effort and without judgement, including lots of praise for the intention even if not the outcome. They continued to encourage him to try even when he got it wrong, and they congratulated him when he got it right.

After three months of family discussion and support, Stephen was showing a real change in his behaviour. He still experienced irrational flare-ups of anger, but he was able to modify his reactions to the feelings, and even calm himself down on occasion. He was confident that with further effort he could change the way he experienced and expressed anger.

Some tips on developing empathy

Empathy is essentially the ability to put yourself in someone else's shoes – to understand the point of view of another, even when it conflicts with your own. It is another of the areas many parents feel their child will develop when they are ready. To some extent this is appropriate – empathy is developed rather than being innate – but it isn't developed without help. Many of us were raised with stories that demonstrate clear morals – the good guys winning and the bad guys being punished – and these passed-down tales helped generations of children to develop empathy and understanding of others. The Victorians were particularly fond of stories in which the virtues were rewarded in material as well as in emotional terms. Today, we have very different heroes and heroines – they are still righting wrongs, but sometimes with little regard for the feelings of others; too often human life is portrayed as disposable, and even films certified for younger viewers show death and destruction (albeit without any blood) on a large scale. We are not encouraged to think of the casualties as having families or loved ones, of being grieved for or missed. They are merely scenery – a part of the plot. It is therefore no wonder that so many children and young people in our society show little regard for people that they do not know. We do not mean to suggest that all young people are selfish or lack empathy – there have never been so many young people involved in projects, many on an international basis, to help and support others, and many young adults give their time and energies to creating better lives for others. But at the same time, huge numbers do not.

In essence, encouraging empathy is simple. It involves asking questions such as, 'How do you think she feels?' Or, 'Why do you think he reacted that way?' Or, 'What do you think she will do when she finds out what he said?' Does this sound familiar? If it sounds like the dialogue from a soap opera, that's not a coincidence, because the best place we have ever found for developing empathy with young adults is watching a soap opera on television.

It doesn't have to be a soap, of course. A drama of any kind – a reality show or a shared book – provides opportunities to observe people behaving in a range of ways to each other, without any personal attachment or investment in the outcome. It is much harder to get a young person to empathise with a sibling who has just borrowed their best T-shirt than it is to get them to empathise with a character on television in exactly the same situation; in one setting they are emotionally involved and in the other they aren't. Being emotionally involved in anything has a habit of clouding our judgements and reactions.

The beauty of using watching television as a learning tool is that no matter how old your children are they will still be willing to do it with you. So, have a movie night now and again, and watch something that encourages discussion (not just you passing judgement) and different viewpoints. You might be surprised by the relatively simplistic way in which many young adults see the world. They haven't yet learnt that situations, particularly those that involve human emotion, are seldom either/or – and nor are the possible solutions or outcomes.

A note on nagging

For some people this will be a revelation, so prepare yourself: nagging doesn't work. It never has and it never will, so there is no point in doing it. The reason why people nag is: (a) that's how their parent did/does it; or (b) no one is listening, so you keep on going.

If you nag because you were nagged, think back. How did it feel? How did you react? There is evidence to show that men in particular have the ability to tune out higher pitched voices, and when women nag, their voices tend to go up in pitch. It is true that men nag too – but the outcome is more likely to be the start of a row.

If no one is listening to you, repetition will not help – they will listen less; especially if you follow the classic nagging pattern of extrapolating whatever it is you are talking about and dramatising it into the future.

One of the most spectacular nags Gill ever witnessed was when a mother berated her son for leaving pizza crusts on the floor, which a few minutes later became the prospect of a world overrun by giant rats which were feeding on babies – all this hapless young man's fault.

Far better is to state what you think and then make a request; for example, 'I think that pizza crust should not be left on the floor, and I feel angry that you are leaving them there for so long. Please pick them up and put them in the bin as soon as you have finished eating.' All said in a calm and direct way, with eye contact, and when the action has been completed, a smile and a thank you.

Assertive parenting

Being an assertive parent means never giving up when the going gets tough. It also means, whenever possible, talking calmly and clearly, expressing how you feel without blame and asking for change where necessary with clear explanation. It is a style of parenting that is much in favour at the moment, but it is really best suited to parenting young people from their mid-teens onward. Contrary to popular belief, it is not particularly suitable for younger children who have not yet developed the concepts required for abstract reasoning in relation to behaviour. Even many teens have not yet fully developed these and may not do so until their early twenties.

Parenting a young adult can be trying, because they do not have to listen any more. There are no sanctions you can hold over them or punishments you can mete out. Although you may withdraw some privileges such as the use of the car, or even their allowance, if they have one, generally speaking it is a matter of talking adult to adult. Admittedly, you have more experience of the world and more understanding of human behaviour (even though they may feel that they do) but they have a greater understanding of their own circle and life within it, so it is important to maintain a relationship based on listening without judgement, making suggestions or asking questions to stimulate thought and offering support. The best way of getting young people to accept support is by sometimes being the one who asks for it, and so making the relationship more equal.

One of the most powerful ways in which we can parent young adults is by operating as a role model. Telling them not to take drugs while regularly drinking alcohol ourselves will be seen as hypocritical; explaining to them the qualities of a good relationship while shouting at our partner for a minor irritation will lead them to dismiss any advice given. What we say does not matter very much at all. What we ask can be powerful, and what we do is very influential.

LIFE SKILLS FOR YOU

Just as with the parenting section above, we ask you to consider life skills under two headings: practical and emotional/social.

When someone leaves home everything changes. Whether the change is temporary or permanent, the impact will affect everyone; even the family pets will notice a difference.

Families are created out of an interplay between roles and personalities, and when one is missing everyone else changes a little too. Sometimes a child will blossom in unexpected ways when a sibling leaves, or a previous harmony can become strained and distant when a young person who took the role of appeaser moves out – suddenly there is no one to keep the peace or smooth ruffled feathers. Or perhaps life becomes easier and more cheerful, without constant bickering or defiance. Whatever the circumstance, things will change.

Discover a new way forward

Many of the ways in which the family functions from day to day will need to be amended to take into account the core changes. This might mean the washing-up rota will need to be altered or it might mean different options on family film night. It may even make life simpler, with one less point of view to be considered.

The immediate feeling when someone has left is that something is missing – that something has been lost. Take this opportunity to bring the whole family together to re-examine how you can all operate, what matters and what needs to, or can be, changed to make things better. All change offers opportunity, even though the immediate overriding emotion may be one of sadness at the loss.

You might even have a family meeting at which you identify both the good and bad points arising from the change, so that both are aired and feelings are made clear. You will be sure to notice that one of the great gains for you is increased time, and for the family increased space.

If you allow yourself to have it, there may be more time for you now. All that time spent running a taxi service will no longer be needed; all the hours spent discussing the future/courses/money is no longer required, as your young person is busy getting on with what was agreed. Before you reinvest that time elsewhere, make some promises to yourself about how you will use it. Every busy parent can use one hour three times over and still never get everything done. Allow that you cannot complete everything, and set aside a couple of hours extra a week just for you. You could consider enrolling in an exercise class or taking a practical course of some kind. Is there time to read more? Could you book a monthly massage? How about some counselling or training? Is there more time to catch up with friends? What is it that you always said you would do if you had a little more time? Do some of it now.

Here's a wish list to help you on the way. Take a few minutes to think about the answers but notice what pops into your mind – even if you dismiss it.

If I had more time:

One thing I would like to do more of is:

One thing I used to enjoy but haven't done for ages is:

One person I would like to spend more time with/get to know is:

One new thing I'd like to learn is:

One way I'd treat myself is:

It is time to start looking at what affirms your life and makes it richer, as these are the things to cherish and develop. So often parents 'fill the time' with meaningless chores, because they have got into the habit of doing things a certain way. A parent may well clean and tidy an absented room or even wash the missing young person's laundry sent home at regular intervals. We even heard of a mother who cooked all her son's food in batches to be sent to him labelled with the days of the week. It's a safe bet that he didn't eat most of it. Some things need to be left behind, but many others will develop in new directions if you let them. If it is something that you are doing because it stimulates you (rather than comforts you), then go for it.

There may be some activities that you took on because of your children, and for which your motivation may change once they are no longer there. For many years, Alison ran a teenage discussion group and said that it got easier and more rewarding when her own children had left to go on to university. She also relates the story of a friend who, as a music teacher, set up a youth orchestra, which she found she enjoyed so much more once her own children had moved on.

Rethinking household space

The other big difference will be in space. Most families long for more space, and when one member moves out, somehow the space is soon swallowed up and family life is almost as crowded as before. Don't rush into reallocating it; take time to think it through. Of course, you will want to have their room ready for them when they come home for weekends and breaks, but it is unrealistic to expect everything to stay exactly the same unless you have lots of space to spare. Before they leave, involve them in certain decisions about their room and possessions. Perhaps they could pack the things they are leaving behind in boxes to be stored in an attic or garage. Perhaps they could have a big clear out. Although they will be excited about the change in their lives, they will probably also feel uncertain and sad at leaving – and they will need to be reassured that they can never be supplanted in our hearts. Young people who hang on desperately to the four walls they grew up in are usually afraid that they will not be missed or welcomed back. Take every opportunity to let them know how loved they are. Reflect with them your happy memories from the past, perhaps creating a scrapbook to take with them to remind them how much you love them (don't let them fool you – they may act cool or embarrassed by your affection, but in reality it will be appreciated).

Keep your young adult consulted about the room use, as they will care what happens, and particularly so in the early days away from home. When you have decided what is to be done, take time to do it rather than rushing in. This is a time for reflection and to explore the associated feelings. We are conditioned into wanting only happy and comfortable feelings, but it's important sometimes to feel sadness too. When we cut ourselves off from some of our feelings, we tend to numb it all down rather than just dealing with the bits we don't like. This is why sometimes people who are 'coping' with difficult or distressing events can feel disconnected from joy and happiness too. Allowing yourself time to work through changes bit by bit allows the feelings to settle and feel real. There will probably be moments of sadness and loss, but perhaps also hopeful and exciting new plans to be hatched side by side.

QUESTIONS AND ANSWERS

Q: 'How can you say nagging doesn't work? With some people it's the only thing that does work! I got my son to university, because I made him work hard to get the A-level grades needed, and then the moment my back was turned he dropped out and started living in a flat with a group of undesirables. I barely see him. He is living on benefits and a total betrayer of the efforts I put into him over the years.'

A: Nagging doesn't work, and I think you have proved this. Perhaps it was your constant reminders about what he needed to do (a polite way of referring to nagging) that prevented him from developing a fully developed sense of personal responsibility – because you did it for him. It's his own voice he needs to hear in his head telling him what needs doing; an external voice is much easier to ignore.

Can you rebuild a relationship with him, perhaps meeting in an non-contentious, third-party location like a café or park? He may be responding right now to feeling free from being told what to do, so go carefully on the instructions. If you want to be in touch, you will have to accept that he is an independent young person, and perhaps relishing freedom for the first time.

Q: 'My son can't even boil an egg. I have tried to show him, but he says he's not interested, and the nearest he gets to cooking is ordering a takeaway. How can I get him to cook?'

A: Look at the motivation he has to cook. If you are teaching your children by standing over them and watching the process, it may reduce their motivation and feel very critical and dull. Cooking is best acquired through a series of learnt concepts interpreted creatively.

Does his not cooking mean you do it instead? This offers him no incentive to do it himself. Instead, buy him a basic cookbook, and say that from now on every Wednesday is his cooking night. Discuss with him how to divide the process into stages: first, deciding what he will cook and buying the ingredients, planning a whole meal, doing so on a budget and organising the shopping.

Sometimes, introducing an element of good-natured competition can help within families, seeing who can produce the best meal or course, although not if this is going to lead to unkindness or over-competitiveness. Get them to host a meal for their friends for which they plan and cook. Explain that being able to cook a meal for your girlfriend/boyfriend is really attractive. Give them lots of kudos and praise for what they achieve.

Q: 'My daughter will argue about anything, she does not like sharing, and I worry about how she will get on at university.'
A: Arguing with your siblings is not the same thing as arguing with others. Often relationships with siblings provide practice in getting on with others, negotiating and trying things out. Try a conversation with her about how living with other people will be for her and how this will feel. By all means offer insights if you think they may be helpful, but you can't sort this out for her. Avoid any kind of criticism of her current behaviour, as this will shut her down. Try to prepare her as much as possible by modelling the kind of responses that are appropriate in a shared household, and make sure she gets what you are trying to do. Talk to her about compromise, why it works well when you don't want to alienate someone and how to do it. Encourage her to notice and think about the outcomes of an incident, and the trigger points that produced it.

Q: 'My son is sharing a flat at university with two others, for which we are paying rent. One of his flatmates gets his rent paid by his parents, the third has to fund it himself. There are three bedrooms, two double and one single. As my son was the last to arrive he ended up with the smallest room, but now that they are planning to stay for a second year, his flatmates seem reluctant to change around, to give him a larger room. They are all paying the same rent, so it seems to him and us that this is not fair.'
A: It's his problem, not yours. Help him to negotiate with his flatmates, and find times to discuss rather than laying down rules that cannot be agreed. If he is not able to sort it out for himself, let it rest and make sure you don't make it the first thing you refer to when speaking to him or, even worse, keep harping back to it to make him feel a failure. Don't ring the night he goes back with a question – rather, later ask, 'Did you ever sort out that problem

over rooms?' The issue over who is paying the rent is not really relevant.

Q: 'My son is going to university next year and my other two children are negotiating over his room. I am the only one without a bit of space of my own (my husband gets plenty of this at work) and I have thought for some time that I would like a studio in which to paint within the house. What should I do?'

A: You have every right to think about this rather than the children assuming they decide who gets which room, but it will work best if you talk it through together. Discuss your various needs (yours for the right light?) and negotiable solutions, making sure you still provide space for the child who has gone away to come back to. The room will need a bed and storage space, so a dual purpose for the largest room available seems sensible – you can use it and your son can too, when he comes back. Or perhaps something from which all the family could benefit, such as a home gym? It's easy to find equipment on eBay pretty cheaply. Negotiate, because in the process you will show them how to do so too – and hence develop their own ability to get on with others.

CHAPTER 3

Choosing Directions

One of the first questions a child is ever asked is, 'What do you want to be when you grow up?' I have yet to hear a child say they'd like to be a part-time assistant in a shoe shop or an accounts supervisor for an online bookshop. There are certain jobs we all know about, such as doctor, nurse, teacher, fire-fighter, soldier, train driver, pop star or police officer. For many of us, choosing our path through education and training towards our future work has little to do with an understanding of the way employment operates, the diversity of roles it offers and the honest appraisal of our own strengths and weaknesses – and more to do with what took our fancy when we were little. Maybe it sounded good, exciting or glamorous; maybe we thought we'd make a lot of money; maybe we thought we could help others and change the world.

A CAREER PATH AND WORK FOR
YOUR YOUNG PERSON

Schools now do a lot to help young people understand more about work and their options. There is less emphasis on named careers and far more on broad areas of work, such as health, education, social services, business and commerce, media, performing arts, sports, IT and computing or manual trades. With a role for life no longer a certainty, the notion of direction rather than career is often highlighted. But just as not everyone grasps French, so not everyone grasps the ideas explored through careers and vocational education. It is sometimes a cause for concern for parents and educators that many young people when asked what direction they wish to follow simply say they want to be famous; particularly when on further investigation there is often no understanding or desire to be famous for any particular element, deed or skill – just to be a celebrity. To be fair to them, however, we do live in a society where being famous without being exceptional is possible, and a whole industry exists around creating and maintaining celebrity – new options for fame without talent have opened up through reality television programmes.

Preparing for the world of work

Although schools do have work-experience programmes, this is only for two weeks and the placement might be with a friend of the family. Work experience usually consists of very menial or even 'made-up' work with low expectations and with little sense of how the role fits in with the wider purpose of the organisation. Most young people enjoy it, both as a new experience and a break from school, but it is not truly providing a realistic experience of the workplace.

Many young people take on Saturday or part-time jobs at the weekends, and it's a good idea to encourage this as excellent preparation for work later on. If your young person has got to the age of 16 and never worked, now is the time to get started – and it does not matter what they do. It helps them to understand:

- The difficulties of working with the public.

- The importance of being able to take instructions.

- The value of being treated as a responsible and employable person and not a child, and returning that trust by behaving in a responsible manner.

- The benefits of knowing that they are a valued part of a team regardless of how menial their role might be.

- Training in whatever role they are given.

Having a regular job also requires the development of a responsible attitude. If you are working, you can't stay up all night if you have to go to work the next morning and carry out the job effectively. What is more, people tend to be much more responsible with money they have earned themselves, as they know how long it has taken to acquire.

The influence of parents

As a parent it can be very difficult to dissuade a young person from a chosen path or to encourage them along another. With our wise and worldly experience we so often feel we know better what would suit our child or where they would excel. After years of observation we are pretty clear about what makes them happy and, with our informed view of the workings of the world, we have a good idea what niche they should ease themselves into.

Many of us are also excited to have another go – perhaps we feel we messed up our own choices, so parenting offers the handy opportunity of getting it right this time, albeit for our children. How very frustrating it is when they won't listen. With our huge knowledge and hindsight, as well as a healthy dollop of regret, most of us in our more maudlin moments can design for ourselves a very different life path if we only had the chance to do it all again. I have met many young people whose parents were encouraging their child to take more risks with the future than they did themselves and I have met others whose parents were trying to tie them down as early as possible to a detailed career plan in order to eliminate the uncertainties they had experienced. Unfortunately, each life only gets to be lived once and everyone needs to make his or her own choices. We must recognise that when our children are making choices, our influence can be overwhelming. Wanting to please us, wanting social regard, wanting an easy life, wanting to improve the lot of others – all of these may complicate the process of making choices, as 'wants' may overpower or overshadow reality.

It's hard to choose what you *should* do over what you *want* to do; to choose logic over emotion or head over heart. Perhaps the most sensible option for a parent is to help their child see all the options open to them and to engage them in a process of reflection and exploration. This will hopefully help them identify an initial direction sufficiently stimulating and enjoyable to prove rewarding. Given that careers seldom last a lifetime, it's sensible to encourage the choice of options that permit a range of directions later on.

How to prepare to support your young person in planning their future career

Before you begin to talk to them about their future options you need to realise a few things:

- They have been thinking about this since they were very small and may still have childhood notions in place.

- Your spoken opinion matters not one bit. Just as you know them, they know you, and all your bluff; 'I don't care if you want to be a road sweeper as long as you are happy' cuts no ice with them, if they are well aware that you have secretly harboured the desire that they will achieve public success.

- Role models are surprisingly important. Many people choose their direction in life because of someone they admire or aspire to be like. In today's world this may also include lifestyle or income-informing choices – and their choice of icon may not be yours.

- A considerable number of young people have no idea how they want to spend their working lives and, given a choice, some of them would rather not work at all. This does not mean that they are lazy – they may surprise you at a later date – and they may find their own way to shine.

- Decisions about the future are never made completely independently when you are still living with your parents. Young people realise that the choices open to them may need your support and that some options will be met with more enthusiasm than others.

- Some things are just sexier than others, and some young people care more about sexy choices than others. Medicine is sexier than dentistry, fashion is sexier than social work and research into renewable energy is sexier than industrial design. Get over it.

- Titles matter. This is not true for everyone, but many people like to be able to say, 'I am this' rather than 'I work at that.' At the aspirational level, many young people will state a title rather than an area of work. They would rather 'be a teacher' than 'work in education' (there are thousands of jobs outside the classroom in education) or 'be a designer' rather than 'work in a design company or in the design industry'.

Before you even think about having a discussion about their future you need to examine your own thoughts and motivations. Here are some tough questions to answer. Tell the truth.

1 What are you trying to achieve through talking to them about their future?

2 Do you honestly want what's best for them, or do you want what you think is best for them?

3 Are you truly willing to let them make their own choices even if you think they are disastrous?

4 Would you be willing to support them financially if they chose to follow a career path you disapproved of?

CASE STUDY: NATALIE, 43

Natalie is the mother of 18-year-old Matilda and 14-year-old William. As a young woman growing up in the Caribbean, Natalie struggled hard to get her qualifications as a teacher. Her family could not support her financially, and she worked from the age of 14 in a variety of jobs to contribute to the family income. She was recognised as exceptionally bright by her teachers, who helped her as much as possible by giving her extra tuition and allowing her flexible access to lessons. She left school after A-levels and went into full-time work in the tourist industry. It was only after she married at the age of 20 that she was able to come to the UK and study to be a teacher.

Her marriage broke up when William was four and Matilda eight. Her family wanted her to return home to raise her children, but she decided to stay on in the UK solely to ensure that they had the educational opportunities she had not had.

Both children have done well at school, although William began to cause some concern by spending a lot of time with a group of young men Natalie considers undesirable. This has caused some friction in the family, but currently William is still maintaining his school work well.

Matilda has now completed her A-levels and would like to

return to the Caribbean for a few years to work in the tourist industry and live with her grandmother. Natalie is adamant that she should take up a university place and get a good degree. Matilda has no idea at this time what she wants to do, either which subject she would study or her longer-term career plans.

After some very honest talking, Natalie finally admitted that she was horrified that her daughter seemed to want the very life she had rejected. She was also worried that Matilda would make other life choices that would prevent her completing her education, such as beginning a family. At a personal level, she also felt a great sense of loss that her daughter would be so far away, as neither had the resources to visit.

Matilda felt the need to bring together the different parts of her heritage by returning to her mother's home. She also felt that she might have a future in the tourist industry both in the Caribbean and in the UK, but that she wanted to know more about it and to get some first-hand experience.

Natalie was impressed by her daughter's ability to express her processes and helped her organise the move with the understanding that she would return home after one year – at least for a holiday, even if she chose not to stay.

Considerations

Any discussion with you about your children's future will be one of many. Their ideas will be continually evolving and changing as they mature, but there are stages along the way where they will have to make decisions that might significantly influence their future choices. That is why it matters that we talk with them often about their evolving ideas and plans – not because we want to shape them, but because it helps them become clearer to have someone to ask them stimulating questions and offer reflections.

The choice to stay on at sixth form or college for A-levels, NVQs or other qualifications is the first big independent step. Are they choosing a compelling and exciting future, or selecting an easy option to keep them going until the next set of decisions needs to be made? Are they staying in education because they want to be better educated or because it's easier than working and all their friends are doing it? If you don't mind supporting them, and if you feel they are better off in education than work, there is no reason why they should leave, but it is important for their self-awareness and your trust in them that you both face up to the truth if this is really why they are staying on.

The same issues apply later when they choose, or don't choose, to go on to college or university, when the costs can be significantly higher, both financially and personally. Being clear about why they want an education matters, for their own self-awareness and for your relationship.

Although there is significant evidence that a university education is an excellent long-term investment,[1] there is no immediate guarantee that any young person leaving university will get a job just because of their degree. Today, employers want to see a range of other aptitudes and considerations, and in a crowded job market they can be very particular.

The University of Kent lists the top ten skills desired by employers as identified in a wide range of surveys on its website[2] and these are:

1 **Verbal communication** The ability to express your ideas clearly and confidently in speech.

2 **Teamwork** Work confidently within a group.

3 **Commercial awareness** Understand the commercial realities affecting the organisation.

4 **Analysing and investigating** Gather information systematically to establish facts and principles. Problem solving.

5 **Initiative/self-motivation** Being able to act on initiative, identify opportunities and be proactive in putting forward ideas
and solutions.

6 **Drive** Determination to get things done. Make things happen
and constantly looking for better ways of doing things.

7 **Written communication** Being able to express yourself clearly
in writing.

8 **Planning and organising** Being able to plan activities and
carry them through effectively.

9 **Flexibility** Adapting successfully to changing situations and
environments.

10 **Time management** Managing time effectively, prioritising
tasks and being able to work to deadlines.

Other important skills listed were: integrity, negotiation and per-
suasion, self-awareness and stress tolerance.

There are many young people working in cafés, bars, supermarkets and high-street shops with degrees, and some even
downplay their qualifications when applying for jobs, as employers might consider them overqualified and likely to leave or be
bored – or both. Although good qualifications are a must for
many areas of work, experience and aptitude still count for many
more. For some young people, spending time in the world of
work before choosing to go on to full-time education might be a
good idea. They may learn more about how people integrate
work and home, as well as realising what they need or desire from
their career path. It is only when you are in work that you realise
that money isn't everything, so when you talk to them, bear in
mind that following the set route might not actually be to their
advantage – and devising a plan that suits their real needs might
be very helpful.

EXERCISE: Reflection – your thoughts about your child's future

1 Draw a simple timeline for your child from birth to middle age. Put on it any significant markers that have already taken place and any that you think should, or will, take place. No one will see this – you can tear it up and put it in the bin, so you do not have to be the perfect parent or politically correct, and you don't have to please anyone with your answers.

2 Notice any reluctance and areas where you feel conflicted, but also notice what you want for your child and when you want it. Be aware of how truthful you are being and whether you are considering what they would want their life to look like, what you would want their life to look like or what you think their life will look like.

3 Does it look like yours? If the answer is no, does it look like you want yours to look?

4 What are the markers you have noted? Are they to do with work or personal life?

5 What does it tell you about your hopes and aspirations for your child? Is it possible that these are communicated to him or her and are affecting their ability to make a free choice?

Discussing the future

Some simple rules of thumb for talking about the future:

• Little and often is best.

• A captive audience can work wonders – try talking in the car, for example, when there is no need for eye contact, and you can lapse into silence when you choose.

- Asking direct questions is seldom successful with teenagers. Rather, ask their opinions and thoughts about an issue – and then listen.

- Make it fun. Draw pictures, invent fantasy scenarios together or play five wishes-type games (if you had five wishes, what would they be?).

- Avoid criticism, correction or mockery at all costs.

- Encourage them to discover and explore – get them to look things up, talk to other people and gain a range of opinions. No one learns just by being told things.

Help them to consider choices and options

The first step in choosing their educational future should involve your young person considering the kind of work they may want to do afterwards. If they are thinking about taking a degree it isn't necessarily essential to match the subject with their long-term work plan, but a relevant degree may well keep their options open.

Whether they have a clear idea of what they want to do or not, here are some suggestions for areas to explore together.

'When I was young I wanted to be a nuclear physicist. I had no idea what it meant, but it sounded important, unusual and powerful. I also suspected there were very few women nuclear physicists. After choosing science subjects in order to impress everyone, especially my father, I finally had to admit sciences were not my thing. I would have been far more successful in my exams had I chosen subjects that I cared about and was good at.' **Gill**

Firstly, get them to identify their skills and interests. What do they like to do? What are they good at? What do they look forward to?

These don't have to be school subjects; rather, we are looking at exploring the individual.

- Are they good with animals?

- Do they love walking in the country?

- Do they love to shop?

- Do they love to play football?

- Are they a really good listener?

- Are they really good at mending things?

- Are they the person everyone goes to when they need a hug?

- Do they make you laugh?

- Are they reliable?

- Are they quick-witted and good at thinking on their feet?

- Are they manipulative (it's not always a bad thing!) and effective at getting people to do what they want?

- Are they musical?

- Are they creative? Do they find creative ways of doing things?

- Are they sensitive?

- Are they good with computers or other machines?

- Do they like to know how things work?

Get them to write two lists: 'My skills as a person' and 'What I like to do'. Give them time to complete these, a few days at least. If you have an easy-going relationship, they could pin them to the fridge to add to it every time a new idea occurs. If they are more private or embarrassed, they can keep the list in their room and add to it as they think of new ideas. It might help if the whole family worked on the same task to bring it back together at the same time.

When it's time to look at the list, you will know how easy they found the task by how many things they have listed. No one is without skills or has nothing they would like to do. An empty list implies unwillingness to self-review or self-expose. Either their relationship with him- or herself, or their relationship with you, needs some building!

Enjoy the lists together and talk about what work the kind of person who demonstrates these skills and likes would find fulfilling. This does not have to be entirely rooted in reality – thinking creatively is important – and pretty soon a picture will begin to emerge.

Next, ask them to consider the following list and decide which things they definitely want from their work in the future, which things they definitely don't want, and what doesn't matter.

When it comes to work how important to you are the following?	Yes please	Maybe	No thanks
Steady advancement and promotion/ pay increase			
Working outdoors			
Plenty of scope for individual creativity			
Not interested in details – prefer the bigger picture			
Clear expectations – no surprises			
An element of risk – the sky's the limit but the ground can open			
Flexible working hours			
Always learning something new			
Interested in machines and how they work			
Not much responsibility			
Working in different locations – travelling			
Doing something that matters to others/ the world			

When it comes to work how important to you are the following?	Yes please	Maybe	No thanks
Working alone			
Having fun at work			
Problem solving			
Interested in people and how they work			
Being self-employed – your own boss			
Constantly challenging – never boring			
Being with like-minded people – working among friends			
Plenty of leisure time			
Work is work and home is home – keeping both separate			
Set working hours – clearly defined work boundaries			
Becoming a leader in your field – a star			
Enjoy the drama of a crisis			
Expressing your personality through your work			
Can work at your own pace to some degree			
Money – as much as possible			
Being physically active			
Interested in systems and how they work			
Working as part of a team			
Like to see a project through from start to finish			
Every day is different			
Motivating and leading others			
Like to be appreciated – enjoy feedback			
Enjoy organising self or others			

Look at the results

Many of us have an idea about who we are and what we want out of life. It can be hard to change those views of our self even if they are patently unrealistic and everyone else in the world can see it.

Help is available

There is an excellent website by the National Careers Service which has online tools to help young people navigate their way through everything from college courses to job applications and writing CVs. It can be found at https://nationalcareersservice.direct.gov.uk.

CASE STUDY: RIHANNA, 16

From her earliest childhood, Rihanna had wanted to be a doctor. Everyone told her how marvellous being a doctor was and how hard it was to become one. She was an average pupil at primary school, and when she got to secondary school she struggled a little in some areas. She got on well with others, had plenty of friends but little social life, because she studied hard. She was determined to make good grades in order to fulfil her dream, even though it meant making sacrifices in her social life.

She had an aptitude for languages, being bilingual from childhood anyway, and found language learning easy and fun. She loved to be part of a crowd and went to great pains to be as much like her peer group as possible.

When she completed the list above she identified that the important things for her were:

- To be part of a team.
- To express her personality through her work.
- To be physically active.

- To do something that matters to others/the world.
- To have flexible working hours.
- To be with like-minded people – working among friends.

The undesirable areas were:

- The drama of a crisis.
- Being constantly challenged.
- Motivating and leading others.
- Working alone.
- An element of risk.

Everything else was a 'maybe'.

Her mother then asked her to consider firstly a doctor working in a hospital and the areas of the list that applied to that career path, then a GP and the elements of the list that applied there.

It was clear to Rihanna that what mattered to her, and what she would like ideally from her working life, were not all going to be met through her current choice of career. And it was clear to Rihanna's mother that her desire to be a doctor was deep seated and had little to do with the reality of her abilities, interests and desires and would probably not make her happy if she were able to achieve it anyway.

Using the results of the two exercises, it may now be possible to see a potential career path, however vaguely. It may also be possible, as in the case study above, to see whether a chosen path suits the individual or not. Sometimes our dreams are just that: dreams.

Now comes the research. It's important that young people take responsibility for finding out how to make their path happen. If we are doing it for them, it is simply not their path. If they want it enough, they will make it happen with our support. If it does not happen, either we were not supportive or they did not want it enough (or possibly both).

By all means tell them where and how to access information or whom to talk to. By all means offer to find them someone with a similar career path to talk to, but don't do all the arranging for them.

Once they have a clear idea of what they want to do and what will suit them, it will be easier to decide on the education or training path that will best support the outcome. They will need to explore options and can begin to create a file that you can work with together showing all the avenues they have explored and all the choices open to them. Keeping those choices open as long as possible is probably a good idea, so choosing an education path that still allows choices at the end of it rather than a specific vocational path might be a good idea, although in some careers the opposite will be true. Only research will make this clear.

CAREER PATH AND WORK FOR YOU

Once your child has made choices and is on their way to their future, you may find the life you are living lacks purpose – and your job becomes just a job. For many parents there is never enough time, but for parents whose children are no longer living permanently at home, or who may be coming home just to sleep and eat, there can be too much time. It may now be appropriate for you to think about your work life.

EXERCISE: Is it time for a change?

Answer the following questions as honestly as you can:

1 If you had not had children, would you still be working in the job you are in?

2 What did you dream of doing when you were still at school?

3 If you could have any job in the world, what would it be?

4 If you did not need the money, what would you do with your time?

Sometimes our lives are far from where we might fantasise them being. Part of being an adult is putting our fantasies away while we get on with the real business of raising a family to be successful, happy and self-actualising young adults. And although the fantasy may now feel outrageous, acknowledging it and thinking about it again might also awaken a desire for change. If the fantasy was to be an opera singer, then in midlife you are unlikely to attain your dream, but identifying the opportunity to work in or around music might be very satisfying, and may help you think about the next stage of your life. If your dream was to be an artist, perhaps you might choose to work in the arts or to develop your personal interests; however, if your fantasy was to run your own business, to be a solicitor, a social worker working with young people in need, a politician or a community leader, or an aid worker in an area of high need, there is a real possibility that you could make the dream come true – if you are prepared to work for it.

Consider new directions, regardless of your age

It is not uncommon for people to change career direction in their forties or even fifties, and universities and colleges take on students of all ages. There are many mature students taking their first degree part-time, and we have even heard of a man in his late eighties who was studying for a sociology degree. You are never too old to learn, although you may need to learn in a different way, or you may need to break yourself in gently if you haven't studied for a long time.

When asked whether you would still choose the same area of

work you are now in, if you said yes, there are still a couple of things you might consider:

1 Would you still be in the same job, the same department and at the same grade or level if you had not had your family?

2 Do you still get the same enjoyment and satisfaction from your job that you had when you first started it?

Perhaps it is time to develop your skills to take you to the next level? Perhaps it is time to leave what is comfortable and familiar and to take a similar job elsewhere in order to get back some of that buzz that comes from doing well and facing challenges. Is there someone you could approach to explore options and possibilities?

You might find it interesting to complete the tasks mentioned in the previous section of this chapter yourself. Looking at what you want from a job, and identifying your skills and likes, might help to plant the seed of an idea. Taking some time for yourself may help you develop something new and interesting for your own future. Be assured that the process of thinking about yourself does not mean that you will necessarily lose touch with your children. Most young people seem to prefer to know that their parents are getting on with their lives and doing new things – because it lets them off the hook. They no longer have to feel guilty if they don't make it home for Sunday lunch or if they choose to go out with their friends on Saturday night rather than staying in with you.

QUESTIONS AND ANSWERS

Q: 'My sister's daughter, my niece, is getting a great deal of pressure from her parents to apply to a prestigious university, which has a correspondingly high entry level. I think this has more to do with the dreams and aspirations they once had for themselves and their pride than her best interests, and I have noticed for several months that she is feeling unhappy. During a recent day out she told me that she is pushing herself as hard as she is, mainly for her parents' benefit and is so worried about disappointing them that she is losing sleep at night. She asked for my opinion but also asked me to keep the conversation to myself. What can I do to help her?'

A: Firstly, it's important to understand that while you are valuable as a supporter and confidante, this is her problem to deal with rather than yours. If you act upon the information you have, and talk to her parents about it without her approval, you may well make her feel further disempowered – as well as losing her trust. Talk to her about what she would like to say to them, and what she hopes the outcomes might be. Help her identify the ideas and arguments she might present. Be there if she asks you to be, to support the process – but don't take it out of her hands. She may just want their reassurance that no matter how things turn out in her exams they will always love and respect her. Talk to her also about what stops her talking to her parents. If she wants to be able to make her own adult decisions, she needs to be able to behave towards them in an adult manner.

Without reference to your feelings about your niece's situation, is there a way that you can talk to your sister about her own feelings for the past, and how these may be affecting what she wants for her daughter now?

Q: 'From as far back as I can remember, my son wanted to join the police force and that has never changed. When he was five we bought him a dressing-up outfit, and we have all watched every suitable police show on television with him ever since. The whole family have always known and supported his dream. Now he has found out that the entry level is just five GCSEs and has adopted this as his goal at school. We are concerned that he is taking the easy option, and that although five GCSEs may be the minimum entry requirement, places are highly sought after, and his application and future career chances would be improved by taking A-levels. We are also concerned that focusing so much on what the police require means he has not really considered what he might do if he doesn't get in. Your advice please.'

A: Young people often find it hard to appreciate the long-term benefits of enhancing an application with additional qualifications and competencies that set them apart – precisely because not everyone has them. He may also be confusing minimum entry requirements with actual requirements, as well as how they may affect his future career pathways.

The police offer a huge range of jobs and specialisations, and these will require specific qualifications, aptitudes and training for career progression. He perhaps needs to find out more about the way the police work from an employment angle rather than a societal angle. 'Cop shows' give us a very limited view of police work and tend to focus on the more exciting elements of the job.

By all means encourage him to find out more. Whatever the formal qualification requirements for the police force, there are also stringent processes of recruitment, where maturity, intelligence and social skills are a huge advantage – and all of these will be enhanced by studying beyond the age of 16. Given competition for places, perhaps he needs to study the lists of desirable attributes for candidates given on police websites to set himself a plan for developing these. There are plenty of websites explaining the roles of officers and the different jobs within the police force. He might also consider joining the police cadets if he is currently 14 or over, where he will gain invaluable insights as well as early training.

Even if he stoutly refuses to take any of this on board, don't panic. It is possible to take examinations once you have left school and, if he shows aptitude, to participate in further training and education once he is at work.

There are two practical things you can do right now. The first is to talk to him about why he does not want to take a higher qualification and whether this is to do with a fear of failure or a lack of drive. Is he a bit scared or a bit lazy – or maybe a little of both? Gently probe to find out if he is opting out of doing something that feels too hard, or opting for a career he can't wait to get on with? Let him know you have faith in his ability to think through the issues and make a sensible decision.

One further interesting development to tell him of is the arrival of policing degrees at several of the newer universities – and some police forces are putting their recruits into degree courses once they have been selected. An interesting discussion might ensue as to what kind of demand these courses are meeting and who takes them. And if others consider them worthwhile, should he? The difficulty for you right now is that it is his life not yours.

Q: 'We have a family farm, and for five generations our family have been farmers. My wife and I have just one son, and although he loved to be on the farm when he was younger he now shows no interest in going to agricultural college or taking over the reins at all. Instead he wants to be a teacher, and talks about the long holidays and chances to travel that this career choice offers. I feel really disappointed and that he is turning his back on a way of life that we as a family have followed for well over a hundred years, as well as being worried about what will become of the farm with no one to take it forward. It would break my heart to see it sold. I think he's being both selfish and short-sighted. How many boys his age can have such a clear and secure future mapped out for them?'

A: The mapped-out future is probably part of the problem. Perhaps he wants to feel young and free for a while, and not to know precisely where his future is going? Farm life can be quite isolating for some young people, and perhaps he just wants to be among people his own age and enjoy aspects of a social life he isn't getting much of at the moment? Farming is not just a job – it's a life. There are no days off or holidays, no flexi-time or paid overtime. Although teaching could been seen as a vocation requiring similar commitment (most teachers do a 60–70-hour week, and the famous holidays are seldom free of work), the fact that he's choosing a career where he thinks he'll get lots of free time is relevant, even if his knowledge is shaky. Following in the family footsteps can be comforting for some but feel stifling for others. Maybe too he wonders if you would ever let go of the reins of something you have devoted your life to, and so opting for a future on the farm might mean he never truly grows up but always has you supervising him. Are you – or another sensible adult – able to talk to him about this, about whether he has real distaste for the life you offer or whether it is the assumptive and predictable nature of the process that is alienating him?

It's possible that he needs some time away to gain a perspective. He needs to have some fun and be independent with the knowledge that in time to come you are willing to design a handover programme that will allow him to become his own boss when he is ready. Take the pressure off him to decide right now and let him discuss his plans and options. It may take time for him to realise what he wants, and perhaps the day will come when returning to the farming life will be his choice. His reluctance now does not mean you have to give up the option of him changing his mind in the future. When the time is right for you to begin to work less it's not uncommon these days for farms to be run by tenant farmers. Your son can still pursue his chosen path while taking on the ownership of the farm, and therefore keeping it in the family while he goes out to work at a 'day job'.

Q: 'My daughter is bright and sociable, and we had always assumed she would go to university. Now she wants to become a hairdresser. We are disappointed and feel she is throwing herself away.'
A: Becoming a hairdresser does not mean she is 'throwing herself away'. Apart from the satisfaction of doing a job that is practical, creative and means you have to be good with people (and not everyone can manage this!), if she is bright and determined she

has any number of long-term options. She may progress to become the manager of a salon, or even to set up and run her own business, or to innovate in product or style design, and there are plenty of examples of those who have turned hairdressing into a significant business (John Frieda, Vidal Sassoon).

Many young people think only about the work they want to be doing and not how they might feel about that same work in 20 years' time or how their career might progress. Help her to plan for the bigger picture by discussing possibilities with her, and ensure she considers the potential you are sure she has. Has she considered enrolling on a business studies course? She might even be able to find one with practical or work-based modules, which might enable her to study hairdressing in a practical context? Or she could support her studies with a part-time job in a local hair-dressing salon. Encourage her to take a part-time job in such a place right now and to think about what she observes going on around her. Does she like the way the industry works, the type of people, the atmosphere and has she thought about the aptitudes and experiences that they bring to the workplace that enable them to progress?

Encourage her to look at managerial considerations that might interest her – the growing body of law based on hairdressing mis-takes and the amounts spent by individuals on personal grooming. You may even end up considering this a highly suitable business venture, because even in a recession hairdressing is a personal expense that people tend to cut out only in the final resort – and it's one business that cannot be delivered online.

Like all professions, there are interesting sideways careers too, such as working in the film industry or theatre, training others or developing new products, which require all manner of skills and expertise. Encourage her to learn more, and see if you can't share and support her enthusiasm.

Q: 'I am a teaching assistant in the primary school my own chil-dren went to. I have brought them up on my own, and now the youngest is due to follow his brother and sister off to university. I've always loved my job, as it has been flexible, given me the school holidays to be at home with the children and hasn't really required me to take on too much additional responsibility; when I go home in the afternoon I don't have to think about too much until the following day.

'Now my children are moving off and away I feel rather bored and that I have time and energy to put elsewhere. I don't want my kids to see me as too dependent on them either, or that I am boring compared with their new lives. What should I do?'

A: Your job may not have required much out-of-hours responsibility, but you should pause to congratulate yourself on the job you have done – bringing up three children on your own and helping them towards their own independent paths for their future. Well done you.

As regards the rest of your life, this is an ideal time to reconsider your options – and to ensure you have plenty to keep you busy now that they are no longer at the centre of your life. How much income you need to earn will obviously be a consideration, but also your long-term goals. If all you want is to be doing more and doing new things, right now there are many organisations that require volunteers, and you might find that working within a charity offers the potential to use the energy and administrative expertise that managing a family has required of you for so long. If all that empty space at home is going to waste, and given your expertise in raising children, you might consider fostering teenagers for which there is a continual demand. Another option, given your extensive experience in a primary school, is to consider training to be a teacher.

For wider consideration of your preferences, aptitudes and practical options, why not try out the quiz on pages 61–2. You could also engage your young people in the process – why not ask them what they think your particular qualities are and what you might do next? If you take this option, you not only show that you value their opinions but you also demonstrate both how to think about big decisions and not to be afraid to make changes.

One thing is for sure, if these thoughts about feeling under-utilised are occurring to you now, just as your youngest child leaves home, they will surely occupy you further in future. Now is the ideal time to think about your options and what you might do next. Good luck!

CHAPTER 4

Coming in for Coffee?

Parents regularly see their child in a different light from others; frequently believing them to be less mature than do either their peers or teachers. In no area is this more pronounced than in the expression of their sexuality. To a parent their young adult is still, at times at least, the vulnerable child they have always been – to see them as capable of needing and managing effective sexual relationships is a jump many parents simply don't want to make.

As a result of this denial, sex becomes something that is not easily or effectively talked about within many families. Young people learn by example that sex is not something that is discussed as a personal issue, and parents assume that if a young person is not talking about it they either have no problems or no interest! Nothing could be further from the truth.

PARENTING YOUNG ADULTS AROUND SEX AND RELATIONSHIPS

There is a variety of reasons why parents might find talking about sexual behaviour and feelings more challenging than other areas of parenting. These may depend on their own experience of talking with responsible adults about sex – which most of us never did. School sex and relationships education (SRE) has improved beyond recognition in the past 20 years, although it is still a matter of luck where your child is educated and the programme on offer in their schools as they mature. For most parents, sex education when they were young was limited to a couple of videos and a talk from the school nurse, if they were lucky. Our parents were similarly embarrassed and often gave us little beyond facts and dire warnings. Today's parents recall their home education and guidance around sex with amusement:

'It was never talked about in my house although my mother made it very clear we were not to get pregnant. The only real information I ever had was a video at school of a baby being born, a science lesson about rabbits with an embarrassed afterthought that it was much the same with human beings, and an appalling leaflet left on my bed about fruit flies! All the rest came from talking to my peers.' **Gill**

'Although I knew that babies grew in women's tummies, I just thought there was some connection between getting married and this subsequently happening. I heard the facts of life in the playground at school when I was about eight. It sounded wildly unlikely (my father, doing that?) and so I rushed home to get my mother to confirm that it was not true. She burst into tears and told me that she had always meant to tell me. It seemed it was true.' **Mary**

'My mother bought me a very good book but it was quite difficult to read and I never did read it all the way through, because by the time I was able to I had begun learning in a whole different way.' **Melanie**

'My mother had my brother when I was nine, so I knew a lot about babies and where they came from because I was involved

throughout in the process in the family. More subtle issues like when to have sex, how far to go on a date or dealing with pressures to have sex were talked about with my peer group. I was lucky that my friends were sensible and independent young women, and together we created our own behaviour code.'
Rachel

'I was terribly disappointed with sex when finally experienced. I had seen it as the pinnacle of human experience that would transport me and my life into a whole new dimension. My parents had provided a very traditional view of sex – that it was a gift from God and the ultimate expression of love between two people. I found the reality such a let-down and I still don't really get why everybody makes such a big deal of it.' **Alan**

'My brother was a tremendous help to me. I had friends whose older brothers teased them or told them horrible things to impress them, but mine didn't. He really tried to help me make sense of everything, and having someone just a little bit older than me to talk through my feelings and fumblings really stopped me from doing things I would have regretted. He was great – a real mentor.' **Richard**

Magazines today offer us the opportunity to explore the lives of others, and stories of the famous and infamous alike are dished up for our examination. This can be intrusive, but also it provides a valuable opportunity: talking about the intimate lives of others is fascinating and provides a way of exploring attitudes within society. Society has tended to reinforce its rules and boundaries by holding up as examples those who break them or behaviour that contravenes the norm, and the magazine stories allow us to watch the process in action.[3]

The thirst for sensational material means that the boundaries of what is being made available are continuously pushed back, however, and when stories have a monetary value, unscrupulous individuals will pick over the bones of every scandalous event they can. The latest celebrity to be found spending the night with a personal trainer/glamour model will fill column inches in the press far more effectively than they would have by donating to charity or helping a community develop new resources.

The danger of this to young people is that the very material designed to shock and create gossip is becoming 'normalised' by its sheer volume. Young people are not shocked by what they read in the press most of the time and may equate celebrities and a glamorous lifestyle with sexual exploration, infidelity and exhibitionism. The role models that many young people look up to and aspire to are the very people who are constantly being dissected by the press for their relationship upheavals and sexual indiscretions. Without a clear moral compass, young adults will be unlikely to use such images and information to reinforce and strengthen their own boundaries; rather, they will use them as exemplars to imitate.

Many young people do approach sexual- and attraction-based relationships sensibly and sensitively. It would be unfair and untrue to suggest that the images and experiences of others that they are bombarded with mean that young adults are all cheating, lying and bed hopping. Most young people have their first sexual experiences while being in a relationship with someone they care about, although this may not be a long-term relationship by adult standards, and they approach sex maturely and sensibly after discussion about contraception. Statistically,[4] they are most likely to have their first experience of sex during their sixteenth or seventeenth year of age. About a third of young people have sex before the age of 16 (although surveys vary) and the majority of young people will be almost 16½.

There is still considerable pressure on young people to be sexually active, and probably this is stronger for boys than girls. Possibly, this relates to being sexually active as a marker for adulthood and as an indicator that a young person is making independent decisions for him- or herself regardless of parental or other adult views. For a young person who feels that maturity comes with actions rather than attitudes, being sexually active has considerable importance.

Talking about sex

The ability to talk confidently and comfortably about sex is learnt just like any other skill, so if you find it difficult, this is probably because you have never learnt it. Do not confuse being able to share a joke with friends or talk to peers about someone else's behaviour as being comfortable or capable of talking about sex. Really talking about sex involves talking about physical and emotional feelings that may never arise in other situations. It also involves talking about ourselves and others at our most vulnerable and most human, when there is nowhere else to hide and all our other successes and capabilities are stripped away. Learning to talk about sex with a trusted adult can help any young person feel more confident at discussing sex with a partner. We recently read an online forum with young people discussing at what age a person is ready to have sex. The initial enquiry had been made by a 17-year-old male who was not yet sexually active and was asking whether this was normal or acceptable. The respondents were of all ages and were universally supportive regardless of their own life choices, but the discussion about how old a young person should be was interesting. One young woman had replied that she was 13 when she first had sex and that she felt she was ready at that age to become sexually active. She then said that she had not used contraception of any kind and had become pregnant from that first sexual experience, although she did not realise she was pregnant until the sixth month. This example demonstrates vividly what being 'ready for sex' means to different people. To this young woman being ready for sex meant wanting to have sex, an entirely physical readiness. The fact that she became pregnant and didn't even know she was pregnant would seem to indicate that she was not ready for sex at a more fundamental level.

Being ready for sex does vary from person to person, but there are some issues that a young person needs to consider before taking such a step, and some questions they need to ask themselves honestly:

- Is this person really the person I want to remember all my life as the one I shared this experience with?

- Am I able to talk to this person about sex well enough to ask for things to be the way I want them to be?

- Am I willing and able to discuss contraception/safer sex with my partner and to manage the process?

- Am I prepared to deal with potential changes in the relationship and our feelings towards each other that may result from increasing physical intimacy with this person?

Parents can help by encouraging their young person to be aware that these questions all need to be answered with a yes before a young person (or anyone for that matter) contemplates sex with their partner. Even if a young person is already sexually active, they are interesting issues to think about (for all of us).

When it comes to sex and relationships, many young people are confused about the difference between how they feel and how they believe they should feel, between what they want and what they believe they should want. It is a confusing mixture of popular culture, physical, emotional and sociological needs and wants, self-affirmation or rejection and vulnerability. It is the job of a caring adult to help them make sense of this and to ensure they have good people to talk to, whether these are peers, adults or young-adult mentors, professionals and service providers or themselves. To do this, we have to really listen to what they are saying and to ask questions that will help them clarify their own viewpoint and thoughts. Someone restating his or her opinion based on 'when I was your age' or giving a moralistic or simplistic viewpoint to a complex issue is unlikely to be seen as helpful. It is very seldom that a young person wants advice from a parent, but they would probably appreciate a meaningful, unbiased conversation with someone who holds their best interests at heart. Many parents, and perhaps more commonly fathers than mothers, feel that when a young person confides in them they want something – they are asking for advice or possible solutions, praise or approval. They may just be trying to have a conversation with you or just want you to listen.

See also Contraception and Sexual Health in Chapter 6 and Chapter 10 on pregnancy.

CASE STUDY: DAVID, 43

David took his 17-year-old son, Jason, to a rugby match for a bit of 'male bonding' at the suggestion of his wife, as the two men had spent little time together in recent years.

They did the typical match things like talking about the game and other sports, drinking beer and eating pies. During a lull in the action, Jason turned to his father and said, 'Dad, I've got a girlfriend.'

David was embarrassed and could not think what to say or do with this information. He replied, 'Oh.'

Afterwards he was mortified that his son had wanted to share this major life change with him and he had not responded in any way at all due primarily to his fear of saying or doing the wrong thing. When questioned about it some days later he was able to identify all the things he would have liked to have said. These were:

'Well done, son, I'm so happy for you.'
'Wow, that makes me feel old!'
'I feel all nostalgic thinking about it.'
'Your mother will be jealous.'
'Tell me about her. What's her name? What's she like?'
'Are you excited? Are you in love? Where did you meet her?'

'She's a very lucky girl to have someone like you in her life, because you are a special young man and I love you and I'm proud of you.'

David could see how Jason would have liked to hear any of these responses, because there was no 'right' thing he was waiting for, just a conversation with his dad. David decided he would write the things down as a list to give to Jason with a brief explanation, because a little embarrassment now was less important than a good relationship with his son in the future.

At the last minute he found the courage to talk instead of writing and, even though he said he wanted to die, he managed to talk to Jason and read him his list of things he could have said and wanted to say. They had a brief, but important, talk about the girlfriend, a long man-hug and then went back to the safety of talking about sport.

Boundaries

No matter how old your child is they will always be your child and you will always be their parent. As they get more mature, hopefully the relationship between you will become more one of equals – more friendly; however, you will never be truly friends – and although many parents today claim to be friends with their children, we suggest that there are certain levels of intimacy that remain taboo between parent and child.

Although sharing the popular-culture aspects of sex, such as having a crush on a film star or chatting to the most attractive person in the room, are good bonding activities, and provide opportunities for fun and teasing, a parent and their child talking about sexual intimacy is probably still a taboo. Talking about your favourite sexual position, a partner's odd quirks or the intensity of an orgasm are not appropriate. It is not that children should not see their parents as sexual beings or vice versa, it is simply that different intimacies are shared with different people. Sex is not part of the family bond (or at least it certainly shouldn't be), although education in its broadest sense, understanding, tolerance and acceptance, support and guidance certainly are. Sex is an important part of life and so young people need to learn what it is, how it works in the world as well as for individuals and how to manage it for themselves. Just as we do with other areas of development, we oversee their early learning until we are confident they can manage without us. By the time a young person is in their early twenties it is no longer appropriate to ask about their sexual behaviour nor to expect them to volunteer such information without a specific reason.

One of the boundary issues that causes most concern for parents is that of young adults having partners to stay in their rooms overnight. Within any group of young people there will be several whose parents have always allowed them to have friends or partners to stay with them overnight in their room; there will be others who are allowed partners and friends to stay overnight but not in their room, and there will be a third group whose parents do not allow partners to stay overnight at all. We mention this simply because your child will tell you that every parent except you is fine with having partners to stay in their room at night. This is definitely not true. It is more common now than it was in previous generations, but it is still by no means the rule that a dependent young person can choose to have sex at home.

Most parents feel there is a difference between casual or short-term relationships and longer-term relationships, and that once a couple are seen as partners they are given more freedoms. This does not always include an overnight stay in the same room, but it usually does mean overnight stays in the house. For many parents this compromise works well, and although it might result in a late-night trip along the corridor on tiptoe, it allows the boundaries to remain intact and for everyone to keep their dignity.

There are no rights and wrongs here, it is simply a matter of choice. Young people are living at home much later now, for the reasons mentioned earlier. If they are living at home, they will want to spend quality time with their partner in private, but if it is not acceptable to you that your child is having sex in your house then you have every right not to allow it. Your child will almost certainly leave home earlier if you do have boundaries on their sexual behaviour. The freedom to have sex at will is one of the main reasons young people give for leaving home.

If you do feel happy with them inviting partners to stay in their room at night (or even, let's face it, in the afternoon with the door shut), you need to talk to them about a few practicalities.

They should take responsibility for washing their own sheets and making their own bed from now on (even when they do not have a visitor). As they are now old enough to make decisions about their sleeping arrangements, they are also old enough to take responsibility for their sleeping arrangements.

They should always use a condom, regardless of any other contraception being used and condoms should be disposed of by wrapping them and putting them in a bin, not down the toilet. If there are other children in the house, they should ensure discretion in the disposal of condoms.

They should inform you when there will be another person in the house, even if you do not see them, as a matter of courtesy. They should not be having sex with someone who is under the age of 16, and you have a responsibility as an adult to ask if you are unsure.

First love

Another key job of an adult supporting a young person through their late teens and early twenties is to help them manage not only their first sexual experiences but also their first love affair. For most people, this is the period at which they experience their first overwhelming love – as distinct from earlier crushes. It is also, sadly, the period at which they are most likely to experience heart-break, as few first loves develop into lasting relationships or fizzle out painlessly.

When we talk here about first love, we don't mean their first crushes, which seemed so powerful to them at the time but usually pale into insignificance once they meet their first love and have a relationship with them.

Nothing in life can compare with being in love during the early stages when reality has yet to impinge. It is, after all, a major industry in its own right, forming the basis of more novels and films, magazine articles and songs than any other life event.

Parenting a young person in love can be many things: it can be annoying, as they are 'away in the clouds' half the time; it can be worrying, as the giddier they get, the greater the sense of foreboding may be for the parent; or it can induce sentimentality, as everyone is reminded of their own first love. No one ever forgets what it's like to be in love for the first time.

EXERCISE: Empathy – your first love

Can you remember your first love? Not just a crush, but the first person you shared a loving relationship with – someone who was as smitten with you as you were with them? Ignore all the subsequent history and just allow yourself to go back to the first few days and weeks of that time when you were so in love:

1 What was their name?

2 How old were you both?

3 How did you meet?

4 Can you remember the first time you spoke to each other?

5 The first time you kissed?

6 The first time they said they loved you and vice versa?

7 The first time you had sex (if you did)?

Close your eyes and take a moment to remember the feel of their skin, their smell and the way they moved – the way you recognised them from way down the street.

Now how do you feel? Most people still feel a warm and rosy glow at the memory of their first love, even after a lifetime and all the experiences in between.

We never forget our first love, and even if it ended horribly, painfully or tragically, the feelings the relationship awoke in us then have never died away – we have simply reinvested them elsewhere.

As parents we need to help our young people have the best experiences in their life and to hopefully choose their first love as someone they can remember with affection forever rather than with hurt and heartbreak.

How, then, do you prepare young people for their first great love affair? Spend time with them discussing the important qualities and characteristics of an ideal partner and a satisfying relationship – not just that they look cool and sexy and that everyone is jealous of you. Important points to raise might include:

- Being able to talk through problems together, so that you keep going when things get hard and don't retreat into silence, and that you listen to each other.

- Having interests and pastimes in common.

- Sharing a similar view of the world and what is important – shared priorities and values.

- Similar energy levels – it will seldom work if one of you is a ball of energy and the other is lazy.

As well as identifying some positives, it is important (and often easier) to identify some negatives. Understanding the boundaries to a relationship and what are the things that are totally unacceptable; for example (this list is not a prescription, but rather things to talk about, people feel variously):

- Fidelity.

- Lying.

- Violence/aggression – and attitude to shouting.

- Disloyalty – sharing confidences with others.

- Manipulation.

- Belittling or being over-critical.

- Separating the relationship with you (the young person) from your family and friends; you being 'a secret'.

- An unequal partnership.

- Not being an honourable person or trustworthy.

Being able to recognise when people are fun to go out with, good company and enjoyable for an evening, but not really long-term partners is an important skill to learn. You have only to watch a little daytime television to see that many people confuse the two. Being a fun person, or even a good person in some respects, does not mean you are a good person in all respects. It is also important to remember that not every relationship has to be full on. Young people who are new to relationships may well have high expectations of them. They may well be looking for a partner, someone to be there through thick and thin. They need to learn that you can enjoy the company of someone without having to have a baby together. Most of us struggle to identify our own best qualities and what we bring to a relationship, our insecurities and lack of objectivity get in the way, but we all do bring something.

Perhaps the list of desirable qualities above is a good starting point to help a young person identify their own strengths and therefore have confidence that they deserve the best.

Many young people place a great deal of emphasis on their need for a reputation – being seen as a 'player', being popular or being with someone who is attractive, are all often seen as desirable. Many will choose a partner based solely on their looks and reputation rather than their personality or qualities. Hopefully, with experience they will learn that how someone looks is the bonus item, the free gift that comes with the person, not the other way round.

When they finally do fall in love, perhaps unlike previous relationships which were often hidden or kept quiet out of embarrassment, this time your young adult will probably want their beloved to be accepted by the family. Suddenly, you have another son or daughter. If you allow your child to have their partner to stay overnight, they may be there very often. If you do not allow your child to have their partner to stay, your child may seem to have disappeared for days on end. Now, what Sarah or Ben says, what Sarah or Ben does, what Sarah or Ben thinks will dominate every conversation and this may become quite annoying, but a wise parent knows the drill and listens, laughs at the appropriate points and makes appreciative comments – just as you had to do when they first started primary school and the class teacher became the most important source of information. It can be difficult if you disapprove of their choice, particularly so if you feel that the relationship is in any way damaging to your child, but criticising the partner or their behaviour will not encourage your child to see them your way, rather it will encourage them to distance themselves from you. If there really is cause for concern, the last thing you should do is push them away. No matter what you think, encourage them to talk. Ask questions rather than giving opinions; help them form their own viewpoints. Above all, be happy for them and encourage them to enjoy the experience.

This relationship may well be the one that encourages them to leave home, as they wish to be more independent or to start a home with their partner. It can influence their life choices in many ways, depending on their age and maturity. If they meet their first love before going on to university or college it may have potentially disastrous effects on the choices they make or the amount of attention that they give to getting the grades they need. The more secure a young person is in their own 'lovability' the less likely they are to throw away their plans or to jeopardise their future. If they feel secure that their partner cares as much for them as they do in return, they will be more likely to make reasoned choices with longer-term outcomes. If they feel insecure, they may be more likely to appease their partner in the short term at the expense of their future. So a young person with a prestigious university place secured in Scotland may feel that their partner in Kent will lose interest unless they can see them more frequently than travel costs will allow, and so make other arrangements, putting the relationship first. If they feel, however, that the relationship will endure if it is strong enough, they will carry on with their plans and make decisions accordingly.

There is little a parent can do to help their child feel more secure in their relationship except remind them every day of their life that they deserve to be treated with love, respect and kindness and that they have a responsibility to treat others the same.

Better to have loved . . .

When their first love affair comes to an end, as most do, it's time for parents to do their thing all over again. Parenting the broken-hearted is much like parenting a young child. They need to be comforted and fussed over (even if they hate it), they need to be fed and watered regularly, provided with little treats and temptations and most of all allowed to grieve. If they are volatile by nature they may quite enjoy their role as heartbroken hero or heroine and may be the centre of attention of the household for the time being while they rant and rave, or weep, uncontrollably. All of this is quite healthy and to be encouraged for a short while.

More worrying is the young person who withdraws and chooses not to talk about how they feel and stops interacting with other family members. Of course, they are entitled to their solitude and privacy, but don't allow them to shut themselves off completely. Insist that they still sit down to dinner with the family, or take breakfast together, whatever your established routine is. If they have chores or responsibilities, allow them a little leeway with perhaps a week or two off, but then expect them to pull their weight as usual. Being told that life must go on will not help, but having this demonstrated will help them to heal. If you feel that they are not making progress through the process of recovery, or if they seem to be depressed (as opposed to just being sad or unhappy), then consider the kind of support they might need outside the family. Typical symptoms of depression include:

• No longer being attentive to personal appearance and hygiene.

• Poor eating habits that are out of character.

• Withdrawing from social gatherings or events.

• Not taking calls from friends, not making calls themselves, avoiding social networking they previously enjoyed.

• Reading books, watching television or films with themes of despair and self-destruction.

If you suspect your young person is depressed, it might help to encourage them to talk to their GP. If they won't go, it might help you to talk to your GP as a concerned parent. Although patient confidentiality means that they won't discuss your young person individually, they will know what services are available locally for young people and will be able to advise you. A short period of depression may have no significance, but if the symptoms get progressively worse, and show no improvement after a month to six weeks, take advice. Better still, try again to convince your young person visit their GP for advice.

TOP TIPS

For dealing with your young person when heartbroken:

1 'Mother' them – duvet and hot chocolate, hot bath, or whatever you used to do when they were ill. Take it seriously, and make it clear that you know that it hurts them. Don't expect them to be rational, let them cry. Don't say, 'Pull yourself together' or 'There are plenty more fish in the sea' – there's nothing more annoying. Let them wallow in whatever makes them feel better – they may get drunk, eat too much, cry a lot, but this is part of the process and you can respond with love and concern.

2 Push them to talk about it a bit, encourage them to talk about how they feel. Boys, particularly, can pretend that all is well when it really isn't. Don't fire too many questions at them; try a more reflective approach: 'When you think about it, when did you first start to feel that this was not going to work out well?', 'What was it about him/her that you really found attractive?' Ensure they feel safe and, if you do not press it, and really listen, they will probably talk more. Do not share their comments – respect their trust.

3 Let them cry, as this is part of the process; don't stop them because it makes you sad to see them sad. Remember, hugging and comforting tend to stop someone from crying, so don't do it! When they have finished crying (or if it becomes hysterical sobbing and you feel a need to calm them) give them a hug. To draw the episode to an end, make them a cup of tea.

4 Keep an eye on them. If the wallowing is going on too long, encourage them to go out, go for a walk etc. Girls tend to wallow; boys tend to party excessively, although to be fair many girls end their wallowing with a period of frantic fun. If they are 'too busy', try to encourage them to

▶

slow down and talk about what happened, to be a little
analytical about the situation. Try to get them to avoid
making sweeping statements – 'I will never trust anyone
again'; 'I will never tell anyone how I feel again' – instead,
try to get them to think about the whys and wherefores:
did you get too involved too quickly, did he/she feel
trapped, were they overly keen?

5 Understand that although you have a wealth of experience,
they will need to get most comfort from their friends.
Don't feel supplanted – they need both sorts of feedback.
From you they get analysis and comfort, from friends they
get abuse of the ex and dream scenarios of retribution.

6 Remember: how you deal with this break-up determines
whether they come to you for comfort and advice again.

For most young people, time with friends is the best healer
and, if they are old enough, a few nights of alcohol-fuelled
peer support, some caring family time and strong routines
around study or work will get them through.

SEX AND RELATIONSHIPS FOR YOU

The key issue and challenge for parents once their children are
grown up and off their hands is rediscovering intimacy – both
personal and physical. After years of rushing to get from commitment to commitment (or those of the children) there is suddenly
more time and, especially, more time together as a couple. Within
a busy family, roles are often divided up so that one parent or the
other is constantly having to be with the children, and as the children grow older, or if the family is large enough, sometimes it's a
matter of 'you mind that team and I'll mind this one'.

Most parents long for more time together, but it can be hard to get out of the habit of not having time, and in particular time for sex. There is also the issue of one's body no longer being in tip-top condition, and the feelings associated with this. Feeling less attractive can mean that any inattention from a partner is seen as understandable and acceptable: 'I can hardly blame her. I wouldn't want to have sex with me either' is a common thought.

If parents are to stay together once their children have left, it is important they put their energies into their relationship with each other. All the energy that went into creating a family is no longer needed, but it risks finding its own outlet unless channelled. Rediscovering a relationship is all about learning to play again, to have fun with each other again without being weighed down with responsibilities. It is time to find things to talk about other than the children. Make time for each other, perhaps going out on a date night together when you dress up and flirt – with a ban on conversation about the children.

For many couples, finding common ground to enjoy together helps the relationship to grow; for example, choosing an evening class together such as pottery, or dancing of some sort (salsa? tap?). It's possible to find that although technically you were sharing a life that you were not really doing so – that you had become flatmates rather than soul mates, and rebuilding this takes time and effort.

Think about patterns you have got used to that may need rethinking: going to bed at different times, having nights out with friends at different times because of childcare responsibilities, watching different TV programmes in different rooms, having different meal times, having strictly delineated tasks so that it is always the same person who cooks, the same person who cleans, the same person who does laundry, the same person who pays the bills, and so on. With more time available, none of these routines is truly necessary and all can be rethought and renegotiated.

Remember when you were first together and all the things you did to show you cared? Sit down together and each write a list called 'What I loved about you' or something similar. Share your lists and your memories and see if you can't make time to perform those little acts of thoughtfulness like when you were first together, flirting with each other, washing your partner's back in the bath, bringing them tea in bed, Sunday breakfast in bed, a walk in the park holding hands on a sunny day. When the structure that has held you together for so long changes, there is a danger that you will drift or even tear apart. It is well known that when children leave home is a very common time for couples to separate and for the whole relationship and home to unravel.

For many couples who have been together for a long time and raised a family together, sex is not a priority; however, for many couples, committing to a new phase in their relationship, sex still matters. For most people, good sex needs to be less predictable, many couples get into a routine of doing things in a particular order; sex becoming streamlined and efficient rather than exciting: what Carrie Fisher, when interviewed by Parkinson, memorably called the 'you do this to me-two-three then I do this to you-two-three' routine. Revisiting sex means learning to play again. Counsellors in this area often advise people to stop having sex completely for a stated length of time, to rediscover the power of touch and share space in a more sensuous manner.

Many couples find it difficult to acknowledge insecurities in this area; that they both feel a bit nervous about being more adventurous and there suddenly being no one else in the house to impinge on what they do – it can feel frighteningly uninhibited. But if this is not explored, the risk is that you end up with lives that are secret from each other and a rather dull, shared experience that neither knows how to shake up.

Simply being more physically demonstrative to your partner, hugging, touching and kissing can be a way into increased physical intimacy again.

For single parents, who may have found it difficult to bring home partners or stay away while their young person was still at home, the new freedoms can be either exhilarating and liberating or frightening and lonely. When children first leave, many parents experience some feelings of loss and grief. To expect anyone to feel sexy at such a time is unrealistic, so don't expect it of yourself – but nor should you feel shocked at your own disloyalty if your first thoughts are of new sexual freedoms. It's time to get back in touch with who you are, and part of who you are is a sexual being. When the time is right, let him or her re-emerge.

Infidelity

Children leaving home can be a key risk zone for temptation to embark on an affair.

Parents no longer feel needed and may feel lonely and sad, and a classic response (for women in particular) is to go and find someone else to fancy you. For men, a commonly acknowledged time to be unfaithful[5] is when their partner is pregnant. This is for the same kind of reasons: they feel unloved and unappreciated, and no longer the centre of attention. Although it has been believed in the past that men embark on an affair because they want more sex than they are currently having, and women embark on an affair because they want more emotional gratification, newer research would seem to indicate that these reasons may be equally true for both men and women.[6]

Embarking on an affair is a choice, and while you have the right to make it, if you do, or if you feel tempted, be aware of why you are doing it, and what the long-term consequences may be. If your reason is that you are bored, lacking a sense of excitement or identity, perhaps you could make your marriage better instead? Many people find out too late that the cost of an affair is ultimately not worth the enjoyment it gave. What is lost is far harder to replace. An affair also risks more than just your relationship; it may break up the entire family that you have worked to hold together for so long. The disrespect and disdain of children is hard to handle.

Other couples discover that once the children have gone, there is very little left. The routines of the relationship that held it together are gone, and if both partners feel the same way, then a split is probably inevitable.

If a split is what you want, it is a good idea to move on before you move in with someone else. Many people stay in unhappy or unfulfilling relationships until a new one comes along, so that they can jump ship without risking getting their feet wet. This means that the issues and emotions of dealing with the ending of a relationship are not really thought through or managed – and the way in which you handled things may be held against you for a long time. You may also have reinforced the idea that running away or finding someone else to sort out problems is the way to deal with difficulties. What kind of a role model does this make for your future, or that of your children?

QUESTIONS AND ANSWERS

Q: 'My son and his girlfriend are always rowing, and because she often stays over, we are all aware of it, because we can hear all the gory details. It creates a bad atmosphere in the house, especially in the morning. Should we say she can't stay over any more?'
A: A discussion is needed between you and your son about the impact this behaviour is having on the rest of the house. He and his girlfriend need to consider the problems within the relationship and how these can best be addressed. Arguing is never a good way of making decisions, because it means that the two parties are not listening to each other's point of view, simply putting their own across. It is possible that these two young people are too young to sort out these problems, or that their affection for each other is not strong enough. Either way they are not listening – but you are! Don't try to talk to him about their specific problems, but talk to him about arguing and how to avoid it. If it continues, perhaps suggest that she does not stay over during this tricky part of their relationship.

Q: 'My 18-year-old son wants to stay overnight at his long-standing girlfriend's house. I don't want him to. I was brought up with the abiding belief that sex should only happen within marriage and feel very strongly about this. He knows how I feel.'

A: Firstly he's being responsible discussing it with you – after all, he doesn't have to, and many young people in similar situations would lie. Also, he's not proposing that it takes place at your house, so he really doesn't need your approval or consent. He is respecting your feelings, but it is his life. Talk to him about why you feel so strongly that this is not the right thing to do by all means, but ultimately he is his own person and has the right to make his own choices.

Q: 'I don't like my daughter's boyfriend. I never have and I never will. It's my house and I don't want to have him here.'

A: Are there reasons for this or is it just that he irritates you? If there are sound reasons that he is not a good person for her to be in a relationship with (he's already married or you know he has been violent to his previous girlfriend, for example), then it would be best if you could share these reasons with her. Remember that what we ask has much more power than what we tell, so ask her a few searching but kindly questions. Remember that as she knows you don't approve she may not be truthful or may be defensive of him to you.

If it's just that he irritates you, or you feel she could do better, it's best not to make your feelings too clear. If you criticise him, it may make him more attractive to her or make her less likely to ditch him, because she doesn't want to prove you right. Work on trying to spot the good in him if you can, and perhaps consider why she likes him. Is it her confidence, her taste or her desire for romance that needs working on?

Q: 'My son's been going out with his girlfriend for eight months. She's still at college and he does not earn very much. They are both 22. They would love to get a place together but can't afford it. His room is a big one, and has its own bathroom, and he wants to know if they can both stay there. I am not sure about setting this precedent. If they move in, will they ever move out? I was beginning to look forward to getting my home back and slowing life down a bit rather than taking on a new responsibility, and what if they then have a baby?'

A: Think through the implications. Sharing is hard, and although you will not be sharing a room, if you are going to make her feel welcome it will mean sharing the kitchen and seeing her every day. She probably does things in a different way. Are you comfortable with this? You will have to talk to them frankly about how you will manage the situation. You don't have to agree to it – after all, they have only been together for eight months and that's not long for moving in together. If you are willing to go ahead, talk through all the issues first and set some boundaries and 'rules'. Give it a three-month trial first, and insist upon a discussion each week to talk about how it's going. Don't be afraid to put your foot down about things, but also be open to the possibility that it could be fun to have another woman about the place. It's also time that you stopped doing everything for your son (if you haven't already), so there will need to be rotas for cleaning, cooking or anything you agree to share.

CHAPTER 5

Party Animal

It's not always easy to tell how well your young person gets on with others or how they behave socially. The only hint you may have is to gauge how often they are out of the house. This, of course, doesn't tell you much at all, except that they have somewhere to go. Some people are at the hub of their social lives while others are on the fringes hanging on by their fingernails, some make friends wherever they go and others have one trusty side-kick and seldom speak to anyone else. Of course, when they are at home what you see and hear may not be indicative of their behaviour when you are not around. They may not be forthcoming when it comes to sharing details of their own behaviour and they would not be unusual if they lacked insight into their own short-comings anyway; most will fall somewhere between the extremes of sociability. Ideally, a young person should be able to manage their social life and social interactions in real life without needing too much alcohol to feel comfortable doing so.

YOUR YOUNG PERSON AND THEIR SOCIAL LIFE

Many young people like to have a good time with friends, and alcohol is often associated with these occasions – which may result in them getting a little loud and boisterous from time to time. It may be annoying if you are unlucky enough to get the last bus or train home in the evening when it's full of young people at the tail end of a night out, but as a parent it provides little to worry about, particularly if they are with groups of friends, are likely to be travelling en masse, and may watch out for each other.

The silent treatment

The difficulty for many parents comes when young people are secretive or dishonest about their social activities, as it leads parents to worry more than they probably need to whenever their young person is out and about. It also makes it harder to know who they are with and to be reassured that they are not getting into bad company or habits.

There are many reasons why young people choose not to confide in or inform their parents of their whereabouts, while being aware that this information would be both helpful and probably comforting.

When asked why they would occasionally withhold information or lie to parents about their activities, a group of young adults came up with the following list:

• When I am with someone I know they don't like or approve of.

• When I'm having/hoping to have sex.

• When I'm doing something they're going to lecture me about later – to avoid being nagged.

• If I'm doing something a bit dodgy (such as going to a club when I don't have much money, gate-crashing a party, hanging around in the street hoping to find something to do).

• When I can't be bothered to answer lots of questions.

- When they wouldn't understand.

- When they would show disapproval in some way.

The same group of young adults were asked to identify reasons why it might be important or necessary to let parents/guardians know where they are. They could not come up with any compelling arguments among themselves for keeping parents informed, but their reasons included:

- Someone knowing where you are will not stop something bad happening.

- If you need help you can always phone or call.

- If something bad happened, your parents would be informed anyway by the police.

- As long as your mates know where you are people can trace you/trace your movements if necessary.

- Even if you wanted to tell them where you are, most of the time you end up somewhere different anyway.

Of course, if your young person is still financially dependent, as many are, you still have a very important bargaining point. It is up to you as the provider of funds to set the broad boundaries and expectations for their social outings. When they are younger, it is comparatively straightforward to have limits on their behaviour linked to privileges such expecting them to be home by a certain time to avoid losing their allowance or even be grounded for a period of time. As they get older and more independent, this becomes more difficult, if not almost impossible. You can still use your financial bargaining power to request certain measures, but be aware that if you insist too strongly they will simply disregard you. They may prefer to borrow from friends or to lie to you, and neither of these options is helpful.

By far the best course of action is to have an ongoing dialogue with your young person in a non-invasive and non-judgemental way. Talk to them about the risks and dangers of late-night transport. Try to make it a dialogue, not a rant – in other words, a conversation in which both of you talk. Ask them how people get home from X rather than grilling them about how they will get home.

TOP TIPS

For discussing safety when out late at night:

1 Be general and lighthearted. Don't make it a heavy talk, even if it is about a serious subject.
2 Be involved in something else while you talk, such as the washing-up, cooking or folding laundry, so that they do not feel they are having an interview.
3 Talk about options and share your experience of the world with them by pointing out things that may have happened in the past rather than vague fears about them in the present. Sharing a story about a couple who travelled in an unlicensed minicab and were robbed and assaulted will raise their awareness better than a lecture on the dangers of unlicensed minicabs and how to get home without risk. They'll also listen better – a horror story is more likely to hold their attention.
4 Be helpful. Offer support, such as ordering a minicab for them if they text you when they are leaving, or even offer to collect them, if it's not too late or too inconvenient for you.

Setting some boundaries

Hopefully, by the time your young person is leaving their teens and entering their twenties they will have become a thoughtful and empathetic young adult who cares for you as much as you care for them. But don't bank on it – or expect it all the time.

If they are used to you asking them to modify their behaviour, and used to withholding some truths and exploiting your loving nature, it's time to put some simple boundaries in place so that both your needs are taken care of and their privacy is respected. Some of these will need to be discussed and negotiated, some will need to be adapted with time.

Here is a list of expectations and boundaries for you both to consider.

- Where they go is their business, as is when they come home, but you would like to have a discussion with them to ensure that they have a strategy for the journey back that they have already thought through.

- They have a charged phone with enough credit and they are with someone else who is known to you (at least by name).

- Discuss in what circumstances you are willing to be rung. If they are making their decisions, you should not have to bail them out or provide an easy fallback.

- If they are intending to return late or there is the possibility that they will be late, ensure they have the number of a minicab firm. If you are super-generous you might even have set up an account with a local firm for just such contingencies, but ensure that you have discussed when they may use this service and for whom.

- If getting home is likely to be too difficult or expensive, it's a good idea to encourage them to think ahead about who might be able to put them up for the night. Depending on their age, it might be reasonable for you to know with whom the arrangement has been made. If you are expecting them home, it's good manners for them to text you and say they have changed their mind.

- Ask them to carry a small mini-wallet, separate from their wallet or purse and phone, containing their name and contact details in case of real difficulties. So many young people have all their information in their phone these days. If they were to lose their phone or have it stolen they would be at a loss.

- Are you going to wait up for them? Let them know.

- Do they know how to contact you in the event of a problem? Can they negotiate the use of someone else's phone and are they aware of how to make a call without money?

You will undoubtedly have discussed managing emergencies and having 'fallback' plans when they were younger and first started going out independently, but if you have concerns, ask them how they will manage if their friend leaves early or the last bus doesn't come. When plans go wrong, not every young person is good at thinking on their feet, so helping them work out for themselves some options in advance might help them and put your mind at rest as well.

Maintaining a balance between work and play

While young people are still living at home you have a chance to influence how they develop and to help them manage the difficult balance between their exciting and independent social life and their important work or study life. It is common for young people going away to college or university to struggle balancing their wants and needs. Having good habits in place already will help them behave responsibly and make the most of both their academic and social opportunities.

It is helpful to get young people into a habit of self-review so that they can adjust their timetables and arrangements when the need arises. It sounds obvious to us as adults, but many young people find making choices and sticking to them quite difficult, particularly when something more exciting or unrepeatable is on offer. Writing that essay, which has another five days until its deadline, when your friends are having an impromptu party and the person you've been trying to get close to for weeks has invited you to come is probably a no-brainer. Reduce that deadline to three days and some will resist; reduce it to one day and there will still be a few young people who will take the risk and rely on their charm to get a last-minute extension.

Although we might view such choices as irresponsible, almost all of us have been in a similar position. The ability to make choices in the present based on consequences in the future is one of the last processes to be put in place in the developing brain of a young person. There are many adults who struggle with it too. Rather than relying on maturity, we need to help young people develop strategies for managing changes of plan. Teach them how to plan ahead and block out time realistically using a wall planner or diary. Computer-based or phone-based planners, although excellent, rely on the individual actually looking at them, and they may find something more visually imposing easier.

If they choose to alter their plans, try not to behave in a judge-mental way, but rather help them to reallocate the lost time within their deadline. If it is not possible to reallocate, perhaps because the deadline is close or other commitments are already taking up all available time, then have a conversation with them about prioritising and the relative importance of the social event and the work they are doing. When tomorrow comes, the party will be over, but a poor grade or missed deadline could have an impact for much longer.

Encourage your young person to have a simple checklist so that they can take responsibility themselves for ensuring that the balance between work and play is manageable. This might include:

• How often in the past month they have done something at the very last minute, and is it now becoming a habit?

- How late into the evening they have been on Facebook?

- How often they have been too tired to concentrate at school or college?

- Can they spot a link between alcohol consumption and concentration the next day?

- How difficult do they find getting out of bed in the morning? How often do they struggle or need help to get out on time?

Depending on the age of your young person, they will also need plenty of sleep, probably more than they are getting. If they are unable to get to sleep before 11.00 or 12.00 at night, they may still have to be up in the morning long before their body clock would like them to be. Ensuring that they allocate themselves nights out and nights in, according to their timetable, may seem like common sense to us, but not all young people will do it automatically. Having that conversation with them will encourage them to remember why they are at school or college, and thinking about what they hope to do in future may make it easier for them to make sensible choices now.

CASE STUDY: REBECCA, 19

Rebecca is completing her A-level course at college. She has a provisional place at an excellent university but needs to get the highest grades. She has always been an ambitious and conscientious student, but since she started at college she has been mixing with a different group of young people and has found their company exciting. She has recently started seeing Sean, a fellow student, and the relationship is becoming serious. Sean is a creative individual and has a place at an art college a long way from Rebecca's university. They both want to spend as much time together as they can.

Although Rebecca is still studying hard, her commitment

has declined and she is beginning to talk about what she will do if she doesn't get her necessary grades. She is planning an 'option B' that will allow her to study closer to Sean but at a less prestigious university and on a less highly thought of programme of study.

Rebecca's parents decide that their best course of action is to discuss everything with both their daughter and Sean. They invite them both out for a meal in a pleasant restaurant where everyone can feel at ease.

The discussion is friendly, and Rebecca's parents are careful not to be pushy, although of course they would like their daughter to make the most of her educational opportunity. They explore the pressures both young people feel under, and the social opportunities they enjoy. Eventually, they decide as a group that Sean will be invited to stay with Rebecca at weekends and that she will dedicate her time from Monday to Thursday to her studies with Friday and Saturday evenings spent with friends and going out with Sean. They also agree that if Rebecca chooses to swap one of her study evenings for a weekend day she can, but that Sean will honour that change too and will go home early.

Rebecca and Sean are thrilled that Sean will be staying at weekends and so are happy to make the agreement. Rebecca's parents acknowledge the difficulty that the two young people might have seeing each other often once they are at college and university and offer to buy Rebecca a second-hand car as a going-away present if she is prepared to pay for her own driving tuition from her allowance or from earnings.

The recluse

Although the overly social young person is the most common profile we think about, we are often asked questions about their opposite: the young person who does not go out at all other than to work or study. There are a number of young people, some of whom socialise online, who prefer not to have social contact with others in person or who cannot manage social interaction at all. This profile seems to be more common among young men and is often linked to those individuals who were exceptionally interested in computer gaming or online networking when they were younger. Whether they have missed out on developing the social skills they needed because of their isolating hobbies, or whether their hobbies were a reflection of an existing isolation, is difficult to determine. Possibly, it is a matter of both. These are individuals who already felt some lack of social connection with others and who found pleasure, excitement and interest in their hobbies – which served to isolate them further and meant that they did not develop a friendship network in real life to reinforce their independence. Put simply, they have not learnt how to go out, and they do not have friends to go out and about with. When a young person is 15 and choosing to stay home, many parents feel relieved. When they are 19 and still choosing to stay home every night, most parents are concerned. If they reach their twenties and are still stuck in front of a screen, then it's time to get a little worried.

There are some people who find social settings difficult or incomprehensible either because of their lack of socialisation when younger or because they simply don't have the same brain function as neuro-typical young people.

Social learning takes place throughout a child's life through the everyday interactions they have with others at home, at school and through friendships. Independent social skills – to do with instigating, negotiating and managing social activity, including the making, maintaining or breaking of friendships and relationships, are generally practised throughout childhood too but become increasingly significant once a young person is operating socially without adult supervision or interference. Someone missing out on this stage in their development may find themselves feeling awkward and ill at ease around their peers and in social settings for the rest of their lives, as most of their peers will have already developed their skills around managing their friendship groups. For any young person going away to college or university, a lack of independent social skills could leave them isolated and unhappy. It may also mean that a young person will stay living at home with parents well into adulthood, as the family provides the only human contact they have.

Encouraging your young person to spend time with real people is, therefore, important during their time at home. This may mean taking them out and about yourself if they are very resistant, or encouraging and enabling them to join in with other young people locally.

If they are desperately shy, or have no interest in other people, perhaps finding a club or class you can attend with them will be a way of helping them to interact with others and feel safe while doing so – or even better, encourage a sibling or cousin to accompany them.

Finding organised groups for young people to join can be difficult in some areas, but a Google search, or a flick through the local paper, may throw up all kinds of possibilities.

If your young person is a computer fiend, even encouraging them to visit a local Internet café with you may introduce them to other young people with similar interests in the area, even if the only interaction they seem to have at first is a brief nod of acknowledgement.

All young people will benefit from thinking about how we make friends, but the more isolated young person will not only need to think about it but also be supported in making the necessary steps. Help them think about what they might say to someone to open a conversation, but make sure you ask them for strategies rather than telling them yours. You may do things very differently from them and how you start the conversation could feel a world apart from what is possible for them. You might encourage them to smile and say hello whereas they might feel more comfortable with a chin tilt and a nasal grunt. There is also a real difference in language between how adults speak and how young people speak to each other, so what is polite to you and me might seem ridiculous to a young person and vice versa.

A lot of our social skills are learnt through imitation, so it might help your young person to see you behaving socially. Invite friends to the house and chat around the table sometimes. Have people for meals where your young person will be expected to be present. When it is just the family, still ensure you have meals together so that chitchat and everyday interaction can be practised. Have evenings when the TV is turned off and they are expected to spend time with you, perhaps playing games as a family or enjoying a shared activity such as cooking. If they love computer games, then a family Wii night might encourage them to participate.

The loner as a student

When a reclusive or socially uncomfortable young person goes away to college or university it is important to talk through with them in advance how they can make social contacts during the crucial first few weeks. Perhaps the university or college they are going to will have a freshers' event where all the societies and clubs explain what they do and enrol new members. See if your young person can find out what induction events are available and help them to understand how these might benefit them. Many of the early relationships they make will not last long, but it is important for their emotional well-being that they spark connections with others to help them feel settled and learn the ropes together. Young people who remain isolated during the induction period may well feel isolated throughout their studies – and this may contribute to depression or drug and alcohol misuse.

Once they have arrived in their new setting, speak to them regularly about what they are doing and how they are with meeting people. The phone call, perhaps on a Sunday night, is perfectly acceptable for a new student – although once they are settled in you may want to call less often. The odd mid-week text just to let them know you are thinking of them may also help them feel connected. Encourage them to join the clubs and societies available. Early on they will be in the same position as most other new students who do not have friends or contacts.

Don't question them in too much detail about what they have been doing or not doing, as this will only pressurise them and reinforce their sense of inadequacy, if that is how they are feeling. Rather, ask them what events are happening, what people do, how people organise themselves – so that they become more conscious of the social links available. By listing things to you they are reminding themselves of the options.

Go to see them and let them show you around. Take an interest and ask questions. If you don't want to intrude, you can always stay nearby or go just for a day trip if distance allows. Walk around the town together and let them be your guide – even if you already know the place well.

Sharing a flat or house

At first glance, the idea of a shared flat or house can seem exciting to a young person. The reality is often much more difficult. Living with other people you do not know is as challenging for them as it would be for us. The usual pattern is that in the first few weeks they will do everything together, but as time goes by differences will emerge, disputes will arise and conflicting approaches to life will become apparent.

All of this is excellent experience, of course, and anyone who has spent time sharing a house or flat knows that eventually you learn how to have good boundaries and to negotiate rules simply to survive with each other. But the learning process can be painful and frustrating. More than a few young people end up leaving their education because they could not cope with their living arrangements. Other young people get pulled into bad habits and make poor choices because of the people they share a home with.

Although you cannot predict the circumstances that might arise, there is much a parent can do to prepare their young person for living in shared accommodation. Having good, clear boundaries at home, and talking through problems when they arise within the family, is an excellent pattern for them to take with them into their new living experience. Their last years at home are a particularly good time to make sure that even small problems are dealt with openly. You may have got used to the empty milk carton being put back in the fridge or the empty cereal box back on the shelf, but these are the kind of habits that can cause major rifts in a shared household. Talk about the issues involved without blame, simply stating what has happened, what the impact has been on you, and what needs to happen next time in a similar circumstance.

Rather than:

> 'I'm so sick of you leaving empty milk cartons in the fridge – it's so selfish. I couldn't even have tea this morning, and I'm the person who buys the milk in the first place. Then I went for cornflakes and the box was empty but still on the shelf. How can I know when to buy new cornflakes if you don't tell me? I only eat them once in a blue moon – you eat them every day. It's about time you became a bit more responsible around here rather than leaving it all up to me.'

The case of a ruined breakfast might go like this:

> 'When I went to the fridge to get milk for my tea this morning the carton was empty, and the cereal box on the shelf was also empty. If I had known there was no milk or cereal I would have bought more yesterday. As it was, I had to go without my breakfast and that makes me grumpy. If you have used the last of the cereal, or

if you know the cereal is almost finished, please write it down on the shopping list on the fridge door. If you are using milk in the morning, can you make sure that you leave me enough for a cup of tea if you possibly can – or nip out and buy some more. When the cartons are empty, throw them away please.'

By blaming and criticising all we do is create resentment and hostility. If we want behaviour to change we need to make clear requests and, more importantly, if we want our young people to grow up to have good relationships with those around them they also need to learn how to manage difficult situations without creating resentment, which might escalate a small dispute out of all proportion.

This approach will prepare them well for sharing with others. Once they are installed, remember the relationships with their flatmates are theirs rather than yours, but if you let them know that they can air problems with you, it will help them to feel supported through their learning process.

Alcohol

Young people tend to drink in a different way from most adults, throwing it down their necks rather than sipping responsibly. The aim and intention of drinking alcohol for a young person is usually entirely in the effect the alcohol has, not on the social niceties of drinking. That doesn't mean to say that young people drink to get drunk every time they have alcohol, but they generally do expect to feel the effects – that's what they are paying for.

On the whole, the more a parent shows disapproval for excessive drinking, the more responsible their young person is likely to be. The 'My mum will kill me if I go home drunk' young person is still less likely to go home off their face than the 'My dad thinks it's really funny when I'm drunk' young person. By becoming their conscience while they are young, parents encourage more responsible drinking as they grow older – by which time their own ability to make choices around alcohol will have increased through experience. The only way to learn how to drink responsibly is through trial and error, but parental attitude provides an excellent boundary within which to experiment.

Today, most schools teach about alcohol limits and alcohol units (see also page 141). Whether knowing these facts influences a young person's choices in the real world is debatable, but at least it means you can talk with them about safe limits with a shared language and understanding.

Most young people find it difficult to consider making behaviour changes based on consequences way in the future. Cirrhosis of the liver or other long-term health problems feel very distant for them. Throwing up, making a fool of yourself, saying something you will regret later or taking risks with your safety, well-being or reputation are the everyday consequences of too much alcohol that young people tend to be able to relate easily to, and which they can seek to avoid. It follows that discussing alcohol effects in relation to these shorter-term issues may well result in your young person making sensible choices.

Encourage them also to have a negative opinion of drunken behaviour – to see slurring, stumbling and exhibitionism as undesirable rather than funny, and hence as a way of limiting the alcohol consumption. Attitude is important. Young people who think being drunk is the height of amusement and fun to talk about will not learn to restrict their intake; rather, they will be encouraged to go over the top at every opportunity.

Sadly, there are frequently articles in newspapers about teens who have had accidents or been harmed by their own behaviour or their vulnerability in relation to others while heavily drunk. If your young person knows anyone who has ended up in police custody, at the hospital or worse, discuss it with them. Ask them to tell you what they think about it rather than giving your opinion – we develop opinions and guiding principles more when we organise our own thoughts on an issue than we do from simply hearing about other people's views.

Of course, the main problem with alcohol is that the more you drink, the more you want to drink – and the less objective you are able to be about your state. A wise precaution is to always be with friends and to set limits on your drinking before you start, and to ask these friends to help you maintain it.

Providing your young person with some alcohol when they are old enough to drink responsibly, but not yet old enough to buy it for themselves, may be one way of encouraging sensible drinking. Providing them with four cans of lager to take to a party is probably better than letting them make their own arrangements – particularly given that the strongest amount of alcohol for their money may be supermarket vodka, with the higher associated risks.

Make sure they are aware of the dangers of drink-driving as a passenger – there are terrible news stories regularly about young people accepting lifts and being the victim of dangerous driving. If they are going out and plan to drink, they will need to think about how they will get home safely afterwards. Talk it through with them. Give them a copy of the local night bus timetable and a reliable minicab number if they are thinking of getting home after hours and expect them to work out the options themselves without jumping in and offering to fetch them. Of course, they may ask for your help, in which case you will need to decide whether this is acceptable or not, remembering that they need to learn to problem solve without your help sooner or later. There may be times, however, when you can't wait to hear about a particularly special event they have just been to and picking them up may be the way to finding out all about it – while they are still willing to share.

Drugs

When it comes to drugs other than alcohol, the good news is that drug use continues to decline year on year among the 16–24 age group. The latest available figures (NHS statistics) show that 19.3 per cent of 16–24-year-olds have reported using a drug within the last 12 months[7] (2012 figures) – a big shift from ten years previously when almost 32 per cent reported use in the previous 12 months. Of the drugs mentioned, by far the largest used was cannabis at 15.7 per cent followed by cocaine at 4.2 per cent, Ecstasy at 3.3 per cent and amphetamines at 2 per cent. Figures for drug misuse in this age group are the lowest they have been since records began.

When considering drug use for the same age group in the last month before the data was collected, 15.1 per cent reported use overall, with the largest figure being for cannabis. Regular cannabis use, however, has shown a decline from previous years although regular cocaine use has increased slightly to 3 per cent per month from 2.2 per cent in the previous month.

Although these figures might be reassuringly low for parents, they still represent significant risk behaviour by young people. More young people are choosing to remain drug-free than to take drugs, which indicates that the messages are getting through from parents, the media, schools and youth services.

Even as we write this, however, there is yet another legal drug scare after several young people have died from taking plant fertiliser. No doubt measures will soon ensure this chemical is made illegal, but there will always be other substances available to young people and used by them. When these shocking events occur, use the opportunity to start a dialogue with your young person. Of course, you will have your opinions and fears, and you have every right to express them; however, your young person may see things differently, and they also have a right to express their opinions. To stay in the dialogue you need to listen to their point of view and to try to understand the world they live in where drugs are commonplace. Listen to what they say, and how they say it, if you want to have an influence on them. Not only will you understand how they see the situation but you will also be able to answer appropriately any points they raise.

Just telling them that dreadful things will happen to them if they take drugs will not stop them or change their opinions – all it will do is convince them that you know nothing about it and therefore what you say is of no importance. Perhaps the most important message we can give is that using drugs alters the way your body and mind work. For people who are proud of their mind and body, and particularly for students who use their mind on a regular basis, and for people at the beginning of their life, making choices that include drugs doesn't make sense.

Evidence from annual surveys and research carried out by the National Center on Addiction and Substance Abuse (CASA) at Columbia University shows that parents who do not approve of drug use and who make this clear to their young person do have an influence.[8] They may not like or agree with what you say, but your opinion will influence their behaviour. Telling them not to use drugs may be counterproductive, but letting them know you disapprove is helpful.

Along similar lines, be sure to let them know you will not tolerate drugs in the house. If they were (or their friends were) to bring drugs into the house, technically you as the home owner would be liable for prosecution. You have every right to say that they may not put you in this position or allow their friends to put you in this position. Let them know that if you were to find any evidence of illegal drugs in the house you would not tolerate it, perhaps even immediately going to the police. This information can be passed on without it becoming a heavy-handed conversation and it should not be said in such a way that your young person feels you don't trust them. Such instances crop up in soap operas, or in the press, and this might provide an ideal springboard for such a conversation.

Schools, colleges and universities will have policies on dealing with drugs. Find out what the policies in your child's educational establishment are, and make sure they know and understand them too. Every year some young people have to leave school or college because they are found in possession of illegal substances and their school or college has a policy of zero tolerance. Most colleges and universities will be able to provide support for young people with problems around drugs and alcohol. This information should be given to the students during their induction period and may be included in a handbook or prospectus. Look out for it and make sure your young person is aware too, not just for themselves but also for the new friends they make.

Many young people are well informed about drugs, but they get most of their information from their peers. This is at best an unreliable source. Before your young person leaves home, put together an information pack for them with all kinds of leaflets and tips included. Make sure you include in this some good-quality drug and alcohol education material[9] that will tell them everything they need to know. You might also include information about useful websites, local and national helplines and services accessible both when at home and when away studying.

YOU AND YOUR SOCIAL LIFE

When you are younger, friendships are often based on who your children get along with, so both children and adults are happily occupied. Many of your friends may not necessarily be soul mates, but more likely friends of convenience and people with shared interests. This is not necessarily problematic. It's often hard to have a conversation about deep and meaningful things while preventing children from killing each other, and childless friends can be rather intolerant of your domestic arrangements. They may prefer a late night in a wine bar to an early night in your kitchen by the baby alarm. As time goes on, and interests return or diversify, new friends are often people from work with a broadly similar lifestyle and interests.

Once children become more independent and move away or leave home permanently, it is inevitable that some friendships based on shared family interests will change or end. Some will continue, with news to share and similar interests to explore, but some may feel hollow without the children to bind you together.

Many people find that once the children have gone they have far fewer social contacts than they had before – or perhaps they simply realise how few there were. And whereas a night in may be a treat for the parents within a busy family, all too soon this can become the norm, and parents may find themselves marooned, if not isolated. If there is a strong partnership to deal with the issues, it will no doubt be a springboard for change and eventually be a positive stage. If a partnership has seen better days, or the parent is a single parent, this can be a lonely or destructive time. Even within the most loving and committed of relationships it can still be difficult to find things to chat about in a restaurant or bar, particularly if you are not having new experiences and lives of your own.

Now is the perfect time to think about new friends and new pastimes, about places to go, things to do and people to do them with.

Making new friends

It can be difficult to make new friends as you get older – so many people will have well-established friendship groups already, but the easiest way to find like-minded people is to be clear about what that means for you. Begin by thinking about what you want from a friend. Here is a list to help you concentrate your thinking. Put a tick in the box that most applies for you. If there is someone you know who might fulfil these roles – put their name in as you go along.

I want someone to:	Important	Would be nice	Not important
Go on holiday with			
Wander round the shops with			
Talk about the news with			
Chat, gossip and laugh with			
Share cultural outings – galleries, museums, concerts, etc.			
Go to the cinema with			
For occasional visits to the theatre			
Attend a class with			
Try new skills with			
Have occasional coffee with			

Perhaps you already know people who share similar interests to you. The person who always comments on your shoes might be a perfect friend to wander around the shops with, the person who remembered the name of that actor the other day might be ideal to go to the cinema with, and that person who is always reading the paper in your favourite coffee place might make an excellent friend for discussing current events or the news of the day over coffee!

We interact with dozens of people every day but seldom take the step of creating a link with them, possibly because we are afraid they will reject us or perhaps we just don't see the opportunities for intimacies as they arise. Some people have a real knack for making friends and will do it easily wherever they go, whereas others struggle to make connections or feel self-conscious and ill at ease with people with whom they are unfamiliar. Making new friends involves taking a risk, and for most of us social and/or emotional risks are the hardest ones to make. But if we understand that it is hard to make new friends, the chances are that others do too – and that even if they are not interested or willing to befriend us they will at least respond kindly.

It is important to be able to read the signs that other people display. It may be that certain professional colleagues don't see relationships as extending outside work. If an invitation is met with a clear reason for refusal then it might be worth another go. Two refusals and it's probably best to wait and see if they make the next suggestion.

What makes a person good company?

Think of all the people you know. Is there anyone who you feel finds it easy to make new friends and new connections? What is it about that person that makes them so likeable and confident?

- How do they talk to new people?

- How do they look at new people?

- What do they share about themselves with new people?

- What is so attractive about their behaviour or personality?

- How do they create new friendships so quickly?

Some of the things you might notice about them include:

- They concentrate on the person they are talking to – and so you feel interesting.

- They ask questions and respond to your answers – so you feel they want to know more.

- They give you eye contact – so you feel they really see you and you have their attention.

- They remember your name or some interesting details about you – so you feel they have connected with you.

- They seem to enjoy your company – so you feel on a similar wavelength.

- They keep conversation humorous and light – so you enjoy their company.

- They share things with you and are not afraid of showing their vulnerability in small doses – so you feel you are getting to know them.

- They have open and affectionate body language but maintain a comfortable and respectful distance – so you feel they are being honest and open with you.

- They are not afraid to touch (a hug, a two-handed handshake, an arm squeeze) – so you feel that they are not afraid to be intimate with you.

- They expect to be liked and to like others – so you are not afraid of being judged.

- They do not make unkind or disparaging comments about others – so you feel they are trustworthy.

Once we have identified what it is in others that we find so attractive and pleasant, we have effectively had a masterclass in learning how to be those things too. It can take time and effort, but all behaviour is learnt. Those people who find it so easy now, once had to learn it too, although perhaps when they were very young.

The challenge is to use the skills and techniques that others find attractive while still remaining yourself. Learn to pull back from expressing your strong opinions on everything by all means, but don't pretend that things that you are passionate about don't matter to you. Give attention to others, but don't become a shadow of yourself in the process. Getting people to like you is only part of the story – they also have to know you.

Finding new things to do

Either with friends or alone, now is the time to start doing some of those things that were shelved in the past because family commitments came first. What have you always wanted to do, even if you never thought you'd have the opportunity? What interests you and what do you find enjoyable? Are there any skills you would like to develop or explore further?

Most adults find it difficult to locate time in which to explore their creativity, particularly so when their families are younger. So much energy goes into managing and maintaining everyday life that there is little left for exploring or expressing the self. Perhaps now is the time to write a novel or begin that blog, make that kit car or build an eco-lodge in the garden. Most of us have a long-planned project that could now be begun.

If you don't know what you want to do, there is a wealth of classes, groups and networks available to help you decide. You can search online or through your local library or Citizens Advice Bureau. See what is being offered at your local college or university. Even if you do not want to sign up now, the sheer range of what is available may spark longer-term plans.

Even if you have never joined a group in your life and have a hatred of classes, now may be the time to try something new. Clubs and networks can provide an excellent way to meet new people with at least one interest in common and to enable you to keep life moving forward rather than dwelling on the past.

A few possibilities to stimulate your thinking:

- Samaritans and other community-based activities, becoming a justice of the peace, school governor, standing for the council, getting involved in a political party you support – it can be great fun working towards an election as part of a team. Joining overview and scrutiny panels for local government or prisons.

- Getting involved in charities. You can volunteer in the shop, but also consider volunteering for a management role, perhaps with involvement in setting policy and offering your fund-raising and organisational skills.

- Are there local pub quizzes you could attend? Many encourage new members.

- Get involved in the management of a religious/faith group or other organisation you belong to, perhaps by joining the parochial church council (commonly known as the PCC) or becoming the speaker/secretary for a club. Extend your involvement in something you are already part of.

- Activity groups – walking, rambling, bird watching.

- Exercise, dance, aerobics, martial arts, talking to people in the gym, going regularly at the same time and day so that you build up an acquaintance.

- Professional networks such as Probus, U3A or Soroptimist International may all be active in your neighbourhood.

- Volunteering, for an arts venue; for example, selling programmes at the local theatre, hosting in a National Trust location.

- Thinking about what you could try to change in your local community; for example, getting a zebra crossing on a busy road or a community playground. Looking for service and provision gaps and thinking about how they could be filled – getting involved is practically beneficial, and networks you into the community much more strongly.

- Get to know more about your local community. Many offer historical walks and you could consider becoming a guide.

- Create a wish list of things you would like to do or go to.

QUESTIONS AND ANSWERS

Q: 'My daughter became my best friend during her last couple of years at home. We did lots together, and now that she has gone to university I miss her hugely. I am afraid to tell her in case I make her feel guilty, and I don't want her to come home because she feels obliged, but because she wants to. Should I tell her how I feel?'

A: You have to accept that she loves you and enjoys spending time with you, but in any parent-and-child relationship, there will always be a degree of obligation. Think of your own relationship with your parents. Was there a tinge of feeling that perhaps you ought to go home? By all means say that you miss her, but put it in the context of life going on at home and you developing new interests and friendships. Apart from anything else you will have plenty to talk about and she will probably be relieved not to be responsible for you. Further on, can you plan fun activities and sharing when she comes home in the holidays – leaving time for her to reconnect with her friends too?

Q: 'My uncle told me that he never tells his daughter what he is up to with his social life, because he believes she won't come and see him if he's out and about having a good time. He obviously believes that she only comes because he is lonely, and I feel my cousin is being manipulated. Should I say anything?'

A: I think you should say something – but to your uncle. As he is the one who has raised the issue with you, you have every right to give your response. But although telling him what you think of his behaviour may not be helpful, asking him why he feels his daughter only sees him because she thinks he has no life may help him unravel some difficult feelings and help him explore why he is willing to settle for such poor foundations to their relationship. Even if his daughter sees him through love and affection, he will still think it is only through pity and obligation unless he allows some honesty into the relationship. Surely your uncle telling his daughter how much he loves her, enjoys her visits and values contact with her will encourage her to visit with a much lighter heart – she'll want to be there, not feel she ought to be.

Q: 'My son always expected lifts from me. This started years ago when I was happy to pick him up because I knew he would be safe, but now he's 22 and I feel it is time he stood on his own two feet. He implies that I no longer love him when I suggest this.'
A: You are being used, and by someone who knows exactly which buttons to press to get what he wants. It's time you learnt that love is a feeling, not an act of sacrifice, and time that he learnt about the night bus routes, budgeting for a taxi, and working out whether, if transport home is an issue, it is worth going out at all. Stop providing a free taxi service, which is clearly taken so much for granted that he does not even feel grateful – and let him stamp his feet until he's blue in the face.

Q: 'My son is 19 and goes to the local university, so he lives at home. He never goes out, spends all his time playing computer games in his room, refuses to eat with us and is generally uncommunicative. He does not seem to have any friends from the university although he says he has plenty of friends online.'
A: There is a problem here, and you need to help him to see it. You can't change his behaviour, but you can help him do so, and changing things in slow degrees will help. Stop letting him take his meals on his own; rather, insist that he joins you. Don't fill the fridge with things he can heat up on his own, but have raw ingredients that need to be combined for a meal. Ask everyone in the family to cook once a week. Limit his income so that he can't just

stock up on technology. Go out occasionally for family time. Try talking more so that his social skills get an airing. Can you encourage him to get some help (universities have counsellors, and there are treatment programmes available for online addictions)?

One of the reasons young people don't communicate with parents is that they have actually given up. They feel misunderstood, that they are not being listened to or heard and that the adult simply fires questions at them or lectures them. Look at how you try to communicate with him and see if you can't make the experience more informal, perhaps by sharing anecdotes with him, or including him in chat without expecting anything back immediately. Perhaps he will begin to contribute if he gets a positive response when he tries to take part.

Q: 'Although I am delighted that our daughter seems to be so popular, our home is either like a night club, as all her friends descend, or the *Marie Celeste* with no one there at all. She seems dissatisfied with her own company and constantly needs to have people around her. When she is at home on her own with us she is constantly texting her friends. She seems un-relaxed and hyperactive. What can we do?'

A: This is addict-like behaviour, when someone is desperate not to be on their own, scared that she will lose status if she is not surrounded by a group of the right friends and concerned that her friends will move on without her if she is not constantly available to them. This may be in part an issue of self-esteem with which you can help. Can you talk to her about her actions and find out how she feels if she does not 'speak' with anyone for a couple of hours and why this is so important to her?

If she is experiencing real anxiety symptoms such as sweating, an inability to concentrate on anything else and a compulsion to make contact that is overwhelming, she might benefit from professional help from a counsellor.

As a person who is maturing, she should be exploring and developing – and growing. If she puts too much emphasis on being part of this group she may well stay stuck surrounded by these people when she should be developing a range of different, meaningful relationships with others, or will new people be put off by her flutteriness? Can you explore these issues gently through soap opera storylines or by talking about celebrities who are surrounded by people who provide safety but also create a barrier between the artist and the real world? Discuss too the importance of knowing oneself, because you (yourself) will always be there. What people who travel to 'find themselves' often discover is that their uncertainty about who they are goes with them.

CHAPTER 6

Live Long and Prosper!

The solution to the issues that affect us around health, well-being and safety can all be summed up in one word: balance. Whether it's food, sleep, exercise or alcohol, it's clear that 'a little of what you fancy does you good', while denial and overindulgence both have negative impacts on us over a period of time.

In this age of information, we are constantly bombarded with messages about health and well-being that can seem both trend-based and contradictory. Many of us tend to hear what we want to hear, and parents on workshops will frequently mention that chocolate is now thought to be good for you, a glass of wine a day beneficial, too much physical exercise dangerous and that playing computer games can enhance motor skills. For every good news item, however, it is possible to find a corresponding bad news story, and we respond according to our interests. Gill is a confirmed chocoholic and she responded to recent research that suggested chocolate to be a cause of depression with scepticism and a hint of denial. We could not unreasonably conclude that if we wait long enough, new research will tell us we should be eating more chocolate or even perhaps making it one of our five a day!

We are not even going to attempt to offer a list of dos and

don'ts to do with health and well-being – there are plenty of these available on the Web, and your choice can be matched to your particular interests or concerns. We have, however, included some of the simpler government health guidelines and recommendations. As usual we will take the commonsense view and simply restate that balance is everything. From personal hygiene to how much ice cream you should consume (if that is a food you long for), there is a level at which any behaviour, habit or choice is too little and a level at which it is too much. Some levels are set by their impact on our physical health and others their impact on our emotional well-being. Too little and you crave, and craving can lead to bingeing, too much and you risk direct harm either physically or emotionally.

Although we offer what we hope is common sense, it's worth pointing out that common sense seldom translates into common behaviour. Knowledge alone will not determine behaviour – otherwise no one would smoke, as the health risks are both well known and publicised.

ISSUES OF HEALTH, WELL-BEING AND SAFETY FOR YOUR YOUNG PERSON

What constitutes balance? This is a question for each individual to answer for themselves, and to do so honestly. Too much or too little can both be characterised by actions or choices that cause physical, social or emotional harm to an individual, but recognising that harm is being caused can be complicated, and denial is often part of an extreme behaviour pattern. There are young people who regularly have fads and fancies which, although extreme at the time, may pass in time and cause no damage. An example might be playing a certain game or a hobby that dominates their life for a while: collecting Star Wars figurines that take over their room or shopping for clothes that they can never wear. For many young people these passing fads may be emotional crutches to help them through a time of change or support them through feelings of social inadequacy or anxiety. The problem arises when the behaviour is no longer pleasurable but merely compulsive, and the desire to do it outweighs any pleasure in the results of the activity. The compulsive shopper, for example, may barely bother to unpack their purchases but throw their unopened bags into a cupboard. They might even find themselves buying the same item more than once, because they have forgotten that they purchased it previously. The model collector may find that they no longer admire or examine their purchases; instead, they simply display and count them. They may even buy items they don't like simply to complete a collection and pursue rarer items compulsively and at considerable cost in order to tick them off the list. We are not suggesting that collecting is always to be considered unhealthy, any more than shopping is, but when an element of compulsion creeps in, it is almost certainly becoming problematic. Another example of extreme behaviour would be a young person refusing action or choice to an unhealthy level, perhaps by refusing to eat any carbohydrates, refusing to wash, shower or change their clothes, and even (in a bizarre reversal of the collector mentality) to keep throwing their belongings away in a desire to be a minimalist.

A definition of balance would be 'choice' in opposition to considerations of 'compulsion'. Although few people who feel compulsion recognise it as such, it can be fairly evident to a relative or friend when a young person is behaving compulsively. Compulsive behaviour comes with fear, often irrational, of the outcome or alternative of not doing or having something. The compulsive shopper may be trying to fend off boredom because they cannot cope with having nothing to do and the feelings of failure that brings them, or seeking the thrill that a new acquisition brings over and over again. The obsessive collector may find the idea of an incomplete collection distressing as it points to their failure to complete a task. A lot of compulsive behaviour among the young is a method of trying to control how they are feeling about themselves and their lives.

Balance implies making a conscious choice to regulate behaviour: having days of excitement and activity followed by days of rest and domesticity; eating pizza and ice cream one day followed by salads and fruit the next; spending 14 hours having a games marathon with friends one day and going out for a long walk, reading a book and helping clear the garden the next.

Here are some key areas in which to encourage a balanced approach for your young person and the associated guidelines.

1 Food

Fruit and vegetables	Most of us should eat more fruit and vegetables. Choose a wide variety and aim to eat at least five different portions a day. A portion is about 80g (e.g. one medium apple, a cereal bowl of salad or three heaped tablespoons of peas).
	Servings of fruit juice, vegetable juice or smoothies can only count as one portion per day, no matter how much you drink.
	Beans and pulses (such as haricot, kidney, baked, soya and butter beans, chickpeas and lentils) can also count once a day towards the five-a-day target, although they belong to a different food group.
Bread, rice, potatoes, pasta and other starchy foods	Most of us should eat more. Base a third of your food intake on foods from this group, aiming to include at least one food from this group at each meal, e.g. potatoes with fish and vegetables, a chicken salad sandwich, stir-fried vegetables with rice, or porridge oats for breakfast.
	Potatoes, yams, plantains and sweet potato fall into this group, rather than fruit and vegetables, because they contain starchy carbohydrates.
Milk and dairy foods	Eat moderate amounts.
	You can get all the calcium your body needs from around 3 servings a day. A serving of milk is a 200ml glass, a serving of yogurt is a small pot (150g), a serving of cheese is 30g (matchbox size).
	Choose lower fat versions whenever you can, such as semi-skimmed milk, low-fat yogurt and reduced-fat cheese.

Meat, fish, eggs, beans and other non-dairy sources of protein	Eat moderate amounts. Choose lower fat versions whenever you can. Some processed meat products such as beefburgers and sausages can be high in fat. Trim visible fat off meat where possible. The government recommends that we eat at least two portions of fish each week, one of which should be an oily fish (such as salmon, mackerel, trout, sardines or fresh tuna). These contain omega-3 fatty acids, which can help to protect against heart disease. Alternatives: these include nuts, tofu, mycoprotein (such as Quorn), textured vegetable protein (TVP), beans such as kidney beans and canned baked beans, and pulses such as lentils. These foods provide protein, fibre and iron but, unlike those listed above, are not a rich source of zinc or vitamin B12 (unless fortified).
Foods and drinks high in fat and/or sugar	Most people need to consume less. It is essential to have a small amount of fat in the diet, but eat foods containing fat sparingly as they are high in energy. Look out for reduced-fat or low-fat alternatives (by law any food labelled as low fat must contain no more than 3g of fat per 100g). Fats can be divided into saturates, monounsaturates and polyunsaturates. Limit consumption of saturates associated with animal products, or processed foods with some types of vegetable fat such as cakes, biscuits and pastries, to reduce risk of heart disease. To cut down on saturates, make use of the information on nutrition panels on food products, cut off visible fat from meat and remove skin from poultry, choose lower fat meat and dairy products, and where fat is needed in cooking use it sparingly. Choose fats and oils containing a high proportion of monounsaturates (e.g. olive and rapeseed oils) and polyunsaturates (e.g. sunflower, corn and rapeseed oils) instead of saturates (e.g. butter, lard, ghee, palm oil, coconut oil). In moderation these are not associated with an increased risk of heart disease – but still use them sparingly. There are two types of essential fats, which must be supplied by the diet in small amounts: omega-3 fatty acids (found in oily fish, walnuts, omega-3 enriched eggs and rapeseed and soya oil) and omega-6 fatty acids (found in vegetable oils such as sunflower, corn and soya oil and spreads made from these).

Salt	Salt is needed for the body to function properly; however, most of us consume far more than is needed. The government recommends that the average intake of salt should be reduced by a third to 6g per day for adults; less for children. Choose foods that are low in salt, and try to avoid adding salt to foods during cooking and at the table. Food labels often list the sodium (rather than the salt) contained, to roughly convert sodium to salt multiply the sodium figure by 2.5.
Fluids	The amount of fluid we need varies from person to person, and age, climate, diet and physical activity all have an influence. Intakes of 1.5– 2 litres of fluids a day are recommended in temperate climates and this includes water and other drinks like squash, fruit juices, tea and coffee. Some of our fluid requirement comes from the food we eat, rather than drinks – and this counts too.

British Nutrition Foundation, David Tchilingirian[10]

Encouraging balance

It is important for us all to understand the basic building blocks of a healthy diet. The average required calorie intake for an adult woman is 2,000 calories a day and for an adult man 2,400, but calories are not the only thing to be taken into consideration. Young people need to be ensuring that they are consuming food and drink that will nourish and support their bodies by choosing a variety of foods from the main food groups. Most young people nowadays are aware of the five-a-day recommendation, although many don't stick to it. Show them how to read and interpret food labels to understand what is going into their bodies if they are consuming packaged food, and teach them how to prepare simple nutritious meals on a budget from scratch. Talk them through the process of shopping sensibly too, buying basic simple ingredients that can be used in many different ways and will keep (such as pasta, noodles and rice) as well as fresh ingredients. Without this information, many young people shopping for themselves will be tempted to buy lots of snack foods that are tasty but low in nutritional value. Teaching them how to plan in advance and write a list to cover their requirements until they can next go shopping is a good life skill to pass on. Encourage them to cook for you and the wider family, and be delighted with whatever they produce, even if it takes you four hours to tidy up afterwards. One step at a time.

As with all areas of balance, how you demonstrated sensible eating and promoted its value to them when they were young will be significant. Denying oneself tasty food or treats is more likely to encourage bingeing on the forbidden foods. A simple addition or substitution will encourage them to consider other options – so comment as you add a treat today, and then subtract something the day afterwards.

Many young people are obsessed about how they look, and their body weight is a key part of this. Although anorexia and bulimia are still relatively uncommon, they are ever present, and parents should be aware of their child's eating habits and alert to any major changes in their body. Eating disorders (including binge eating with or without induced vomiting) have a psychological component. They are not just about food but are usually about control, and are especially a risk for young people who may feel that they do not have the power to take control over other aspects of their lives.

One of the ways a parent can support their child to eat healthily is to present them with a world view in which diversity is both celebrated and valued, and different body shapes and weights, different appearances and behaviours are noted. And it's a good idea too to encourage them to first spot and then challenge the media-led images designed to promote consumerism.

Obesity too is a real issue for young people these days and generally it results from a combination of poor diet that is over reliant on 'fast foods' as well as high sugar and fat products and a lack of exercise. Although it is true that some people do have a propensity to store fat in their cells more efficiently than others, they still need to be consuming more calories in their diet than they are burning up in activity and exercise in order to store the excess. Being overweight can have serious health consequences that might shorten a person's life as well as contributing to low self-esteem and deep-seated feelings of shame connected to their food behaviours. Losing weight and dieting are unfortunately short-term measures for most people, as lost weight tends to return over and over again. It is always best to help a young person avoid obesity rather than manage it, which is why the campaigns geared at lowering the national obesity figures are about promoting a healthy lifestyle not the dieting and weight-conscious messages of the people who make billions out of promoting their low-fat and dieting products.

Should a young person have an obesity problem, however, it is important to recognise that pushing them to lose weight will not improve the issues that have resulted in the weight in the first place. Many obese people have self-esteem and/or intimacy issues that their weight simply masks – their eating may well be a symptom rather than the problem itself. Counselling and life coaching have been shown to be helpful with weight issues, as they encourage a greater understanding of problem solving and empower the individual to change aspects of themselves and their lives that have become 'stuck' or seem unmanageable. Along with these, help and encouragement to embrace a healthier diet and increased activity while reflecting on the changes in emotional and physical health and well-being, may well enable a long-term or even life-long change.

2 Exercise

Children and young people This age group should do at least 60 minutes of moderate-intensity physical activity each day – but options are far more varied than those on the curriculum at most schools and could include dance, boxing, martial arts and Parkour. At least twice a week, this should include activities that strengthen bone and muscles, and increase flexibility, often referred to as 'weight-bearing exercise', although the weight borne may just be the weight of the body itself. This can be achieved in bouts of activity throughout the day, including playing a sport or taking part in movement-related activities during school breaks, walking to and from school, PE classes, swimming, bike rides, games, and so on. Many young people now belong to gyms either through school or outside, and this is an excellent opportunity if it is used properly. A helpful gym for a young person will include some form of supervision or target reviewing, don't be fooled into thinking this may be only available at more pricey gyms. Local authority gyms often provide excellent support towards fitness or weight-related goals and are often among the cheaper options available, although the facilities may not be as shiny and new as more fashionable options.

Adults For general health, adults should do a minimum of 30 minutes of moderate-intensity physical activity, at least five days a week. You can achieve this by doing all the activity in one session or through shorter bouts of ten minutes or more. It can include: walking or cycling part of your journey to work, using the stairs, doing manual tasks.

An average routine could include two to three more-intense sessions, such as a sporting activity, visiting the gym or swimming. During the weekend, consider: longer walks, biking, swimming, sports activities, DIY, gardening

(Taken from NHS Choices website[11])

Encouraging balance

As well more significant activities, such as going for a walk in the park or cycling 5 miles, there are many little things that anyone can do to be more active: taking the stairs instead of the lift, walking instead of taking a bus, walking to the bus stop instead of taking the car, washing-up by hand instead of using a dishwasher!

Many young people are very active and put the rest of us to shame, but there are quite a number who spend far too long slumped in front of the television or at their computers or games consoles.

One of the easiest ways to encourage a young person to be active is to get out and about with them. If you haven't been on a bike for years, now is the time to dust off that old cycle or treat yourself to a new one, and an ordinary bike for occasional use need not be expensive. Walking together can also be both bonding and active; it's a great time to talk and get exercise at the same time. Dogs are a wonderful source of exercise. No matter what the weather is like, they need to go out, so if you've always wanted one but never quite got round to it, now might be good time. A dog will naturally return your care, love and attention, so think about who will manage this once your young person has finally moved on to college or independent living.

If you can't cope with cycling or a dog, then go shopping together, choosing a big mall or long high street to walk along (in the US and in winter, it's common to see elderly people using the long malls for exercise through power walking). Sunday-morning swimming is a great family activity, or you could get your young person to help you train for a longer run by running with you a couple of times a week.

An unhealthy way of managing exercise is to compulsively overwork the body, either as a way of managing weight or of changing physical appearance. As with any compulsive behaviour there are psychological aspects to be considered, and no amount of nagging or discussion will change the behaviour unless the underlying issues are addressed. If the behaviour is entrenched, it may be best to talk to a doctor or encourage your young person to see a counsellor. But do bear in mind that what we say will have far less impact than what we do so, if you want your young person to be active and full of energy, and to achieve this in a balanced way, it is helpful if you demonstrate the value and practice of exercise, and its moderate pursuit.

3 Sleep

Infants
Birth to 2 months need 10.5–18 hours
2 to 12 months need 14–15 hours

Toddlers/children
12–18 months need 13–15 hours
18 months to 3 years need 12–14 hours
3–5 years old need 11–13 hours
5–12 years old need 9–11 hours

Adolescents Need at least 8½–9½ hours per night

Adults Typically need 7–9 hours per night

(Taken from NHS Choices www.nhs.uk[12])

Encouraging balance

Get them to notice their own patterns around sleep, such as how important and pleasurable it is to feel alert the next day, what stops them sleeping and when do they sleep soundly?

Many of the things that young people like doing are those that prevent them from sleeping, and these include watching the television, DVDs or movies late at night, talking on the phone or texting, using computers or games. These tend to stimulate the brain and so will often delay sleepiness. All of these behaviours are a choice, and if young people need sleep they can make different choices.

Things that encourage sleep include a pillow that stays cool and getting into a cold bed as the brain requires a drop in temperature to sleep, a cool bedroom to help you stay sleeping, a bedtime routine that calms the mind, for example reading, meditation or puzzles such as sudoku or word search. Peppermint tea might be a better way of calming the body than a milky drink, because milky drinks can raise blood sugar levels. Some people like to drift off to sleep with the radio or television on whereas others prefer absolute silence – and this could be the basis of an interesting conversation if you get your young person to identify what works for them by practising and experimenting. Gill has discovered that wearing earplugs is her preferred method of achieving a good night's sleep; a friend has bought blackout blinds for her windows to keep all light out, although you might want to experiment with an eye-mask before committing to the expenditure.

The body produces a hormone called melatonin which helps the body switch off for sleep, and there are several foods that are high in melatonin which can perhaps help. These include sour cherries (particularly high in melatonin), barley, oats, walnuts, rice, asparagus and tomatoes, and many others. Melatonin is produced in darkness, and even moderate light can decrease the body's production. Most people produce it late at night, which is why going to bed earlier than usual may actually result in a restless night rather than more sleep.

Whatever your age, sleep patterns are also a matter of personal preference. Some people like to stay up late and sleep late in the morning, others like to go to bed early and be up with the lark. But although such preferences may be inbuilt, the world doesn't take them into account when setting timetables. Most jobs start at a set time and finish at a set time. Almost everything runs by appointment or schedule, even if it is sometimes late, and individuals need to be able to regulate their own systems to fit the expectations of the world they live in. Everyone needs to learn to balance today's bedtime with tomorrow's timetable.

4 Alcohol

Advice for young people and their parents about alcohol:

Under 15 Children and their parents and carers are advised that an alcohol-free childhood is the healthiest and best option; however, if children drink alcohol, it should not be until at least the age of 15 years.

15–17 years If young people aged 15–17 years consume alcohol, it should always be with the guidance of a parent or carer or in a supervised environment. Young people aged 15–17 years should never exceed the recommended adult daily limits and, on days when they drink, consumption should usually be below such levels.

(Advice from the Chief Medical Officer, Sir Liam Donaldson – December 2009, taken from Drinkaware[13])

The excellent Drinkaware website (www.drinkaware.co.uk) has an amazing array of information, enough to make anyone think twice about the consequences of alcohol. Have a look at it with your young person for some really well thought-out and well-presented new facts and issues. Girls, in particular, might be amazed at the 'Calories in drinks' section and boys interested in some of the issues raised under 'Men about town'.

Alcohol limits:

Women A maximum of 2–3 units (see below) a day

Men A maximum of 3–4 units (see below) a day

What is an alcohol unit?

Many people incorrectly measure units as 'drinks' – or glasses of wine! In reality, one unit is measured as 10ml or 8g of pure alcohol. This equals one 25ml single measure of whisky (alcohol by volume – ABV – 40 per cent), or a third of a pint of beer (ABV 5–6 per cent) or half a standard glass (175ml) of red wine (ABV 12 per cent).

Encouraging balance

By far the most important way in which you can encourage your young person to develop a balanced and sensible attitude to alcohol is by demonstrating one yourself. Being overly tolerant of their drinking will not help them develop boundaries, and neither will allowing them to drink at home as a regular occurrence. As you can see from the information above, the Chief Medical Officer has clearly stated that no young person under the age of 15 should be drinking alcohol regardless of the law, and that from 15 to 17 they should only be allowed to drink under adult supervision. This may seem draconian in today's society, but it is the only way in which the present situation of excessive drinking by young people will be turned around. It is hard to be the parent who is putting their foot down when so many others are not, but rest assured you are doing the right thing by setting clear boundaries.

The astonishing number of deaths attributed to alcohol in this country through violence, accidents and disease should have us all concerned. The excellent NHS Choices website shows comparisons of different causes of death by age group. Deaths by illegal drugs is still relatively rare, particularly in comparison to deaths due to alcohol-related illness. But we cannot expect young people to moderate their drinking because of a range of charts or what might happen ten years down the line. Longer-term outcomes tend not to influence them, but we as adults should be able to do this, and suggesting what really matters in relation to young people's health and well-being is important, even if it makes us a little unpopular.

Some other issues to encourage health and well-being that have no official guidelines:

Personal hygiene

Different people will have different views of what constitutes a balanced approach to hygiene, and we are not trying to tell you what is right and what is wrong. It is, however, worth thinking about the subject so that you are in a position to offer guidance to your young person and to encourage good personal habits. Changing clothes more than once or twice a day (depending on whether they are going out or not) is probably sufficient, although some might consider wearing fresh clothes twice a day excessive. Most people would consider changing underwear every day to be normal, changing underwear once a week to be unpleasant and changing underwear four times a day obsessive. Likewise, with showering or bathing, once or twice a day (if going out) is probably acceptable to most people, showering or bathing once a week not quite enough, and showering or bathing four times a day generally excessive.

Sometimes young people get quite worried about hygiene and are concerned that they may be unpleasant to be near and so wash or shower more than is good for either their skin or your associated bills. They may cover themselves with lotions and potions to mask their smell, and be unaware that using several different highly scented concoctions at once on different parts of their body may leave them unpleasant to be near for an entirely different reason. Encourage your young person to use highly scented products sparingly and to be aware that despite the flowery or natural sounding names, many of these products contain a range of chemicals that are not particularly skin-friendly. Encourage them to think of other people both in terms of not keeping clean enough and in terms of over-scenting themselves – neither are nice to be near, and those with allergies may find synthetic perfumes cause reactions.

Personal hygiene is as much a matter of habit as anything else, so encourage your young person to develop a routine. As they get older, this should include taking care of their laundry and ironing so that they always have clean clothes to wear and do not have to resort to fishing out yesterday's pants from the laundry basket.

Contraception and sexual health

Young people should have an understanding, long before they are sexually active themselves, that looking after your sexual health is part of your general health, in the same way that you should regularly attend a dentist and be registered with a doctor.

Anyone who is sexually active and is not using condoms as a matter of course should regularly attend a sexual-health clinic to ensure that they are not carrying any infections and are healthy. Although conditions like testicular cancer and cervical cancer are relatively rare in young people, they do still occur, and regular check-ups will ensure a young person stays well. Chlamydia can be almost symptomless, particularly in young men, and is at epidemic proportions in the UK. The long-term consequences of untreated chlamydia can be highly significant (for example, infertility). Everyone who is sexually active should regularly test for chlamydia. For young people, this is quick, simple and free, as it is based on a urine test available from all doctors and many clinics or chemists.

Most areas will have sexual-health clinics designed specifically for young people, and you or your child can easily find the nearest to your home by going to the NHS Choices website (www.nhs.uk) and clicking on the 'Find and choose services' tab. Services vary from area to area but will usually include advice on contraception, contraceptive services, sexual-health screening and emergency contraception, as well as general sexual-health advice.

Parents have a very important role to play with helping their child to have a healthy and responsible attitude to sex and contraception, although it does not always follow that they will get everything they need from you. There are more modern methods of contraception than were around when you were younger, and unless you are fully up to date and equipped to provide information, your role should rather be that of supporter than adviser. When it comes to their attitude to sex, however, you are a major influence. If they have grown up believing that sex is something that belongs within a committed and stable relationship between two people who have discussed and made an informed decision about contraception, they will be more likely to behave in the same way. But waiting until your young person is past puberty is too late – these messages need to begin in childhood long before the biology kicks in. As young adults they need to hear consistent messages about responsibility and respect within sexual relationships and to have serious discussions about issues such as the competency of an individual to give consent to sex when they have been drinking heavily and the lifelong responsibility of both mother and father for a child, regardless of the relationship between the parents.

You might also discuss the different attitudes society still holds towards sexually active young men and sexually active young women. Many women still feel that they will be judged by men if they carry condoms and feel unable to insist upon condoms with partners who refuse to use them.

Young women and young men need to accept condom use as a part of sex – even when other contraception is being used, as only condoms and Femidoms provide protection against sexually transmitted infections including HIV, herpes, chlamydia and gonorrhoea. Being on the pill might prevent conception, but it will not prevent the spread of infection that can occur through sex.

The behaviour of other people

Some young people are more streetwise than others, perhaps because of the school they have attended or the area in which they live, also possibly because of their observational skills and how much they talk and listen to their peers. Young people can be very confident about their ability to cope with life and all it throws at them, and this may result in a lack of care and attention to their personal safety. Teaching your young person some simple strategies for safety is a wise precaution; for example, you could suggest a wider awareness when money is taken from a cash machine in the street. Most of us are aware whether anyone is watching us typing in our PIN number, but there may be someone on the other side of the road who has watched us take the money and has noted where we have put it, and people are targeted every day by professional thieves as they leave banks and cash tills. Similarly, using phones or music players late at night can make them less aware of what is going on around them, and sticking to well-lit areas where there are plenty of other people may help them stay safe.

The use of new media

It's hard for adults to understand just how important gadgets like phones, tablets and computers are to young people. Although these provide significant benefits to anyone, they are particularly appealing to young people, who often prefer to communicate without seeing the person they are talking to (which is why difficult conversations often work well in the car, when there is no eye-contact), love receiving information whenever they want it and revel in the ability to record and share their lives and the lives of others from moment to moment.

With these benefits come risks, however: addiction to porn, game playing or second-life sites; posting pictures and information that you later regret; and cyber-bullying. We recently heard of a case where a job offer was withdrawn because an employer resented the way a future employee announced their connection by linking the employer's brand with celebratory behaviour they saw as unacceptable. The media is full of the latest household name to have their private information leaked, and many young people do not realise this could happen to them.

If you feel your young person is spending far too much time on the computer, and they sometimes turn down real-life opportunities or the chance to meet with others in order to stay at home and get online, then there is a possibility that things are getting out of control. You might begin by instigating an honest conversation with them, although if they are accessing a lot of porn sites they may be unwilling to talk to you. In order to offer any help or support there needs to be recognition on the part of the young person that there is a real or potential problem in the amount of time they are spending online. You could suggest that they create a timetable or some rules to restrict their computer use and that you could support them to follow. If they find it impossible to stick to this, or if their computer use is increasingly taking over part of their life that was used for other things, then it is likely that there is a problem, and you may need professional help. There is a recognition that computer addiction does exist. (See Resources on page 240 for how to find help and support.)

There are some simple questions you can suggest that your young person ask themselves each time they post something on a social media site, or otherwise online, such as:

- How would I feel if my mother saw this?

- How would I feel if my head-teacher/tutor saw this?

- How would I feel if my future partner saw this?

- How would I feel if my future employer saw this?

And in each case, what could the consequences be?

Cyber-bullying is a big problem that we feel may have part of its roots in the current way in which young people are encouraged to be kind and considerate to each other on the surface but are allowed to harbour resentments underneath. It's helpful to encourage young people to be more honest in how they express themselves towards each other and to have simple strategies for dealing with anyone who posts unkind or derogatory comments about them; for example, having the confidence not to read their bad press and thinking ahead about how they will deal with bad feedback should they become aware of it. Although it might be uncomfortable, it's not wrong to be angry – but it is unacceptable to act aggressively towards another person, no matter how they have behaved towards us. It's helpful to encourage young people to express their anger and then, once they have cooled down, to think clearly about an effective next step that does not prolong or exacerbate the situation. This might mean sometimes doing nothing or at others putting forward their side of the story or even taking some form of official action.

Transport and getting around

Learning to use public transport is something that most young people will need to do, and although it is relatively simple during daylight hours, it can become quite difficult later on and through the night. Even our larger cities have only limited night-time transport, and more rural areas may have almost no transport after dark. It may be tempting, particularly while they are living at home, to give your young person lifts to and from their destination. Although they may complain, many parents quite like to feel useful, to know where their young person is and when they will be back; however, this is not in the best interests of a young person, who should be developing their independent living skills – and these include learning to make their own travel arrangements. Part of making choices about what to do and where to go is the accessibility of available pastimes as well as other practical considerations such as cost. Encourage them to walk or use public transport, or to share cabs with friends and talk through with them how they will get home from a night out, so that they learn to plan ahead and get into the habit of thinking about their options before they are stranded at 3.00 am.

There are a few safety tips every young person should know:

- Never take a lift from someone who has been drinking or is obviously tired.

- Always use a seat belt, even in the back seat.

- When being picked up by a cab, ask the driver who they have been told to pick up – if they cannot tell you your name, don't get in. Calls to cab companies can be intercepted and unlicensed mini-cabs are just that – unlicensed. As the warning posters say: getting into an unlicensed cab is the same as getting into a car with a stranger – and could be equally dangerous.

- Always make sure someone knows where you are (perhaps have a 'text buddy' – a named friend who is regularly texted with details of your whereabouts if you are doing something different, going somewhere new or out with someone unfamiliar) and whenever possible, travel with someone else.

- Avoid eye contact on buses and tubes at night when people have been drinking. When drunk, some people will pick a fight with anyone they feel is looking at them.

- Check the times of the last trains or buses before you leave home – most timetables are available online.

We are all familiar with the concept of a nominated driver – someone who opts to drink no alcohol, usually on a rota basis, in order to drive everyone else home. Encourage your young person to consider setting up a nominated non-drinker rota with friends, and an awareness that their role is to ensure everyone gets home safely after a night out and remains sober in order to deal with any problems that occur. The nominated person can get everyone to their bus or ensure they are not walking alone as well as being on hand to call for back up if something untoward happens. This may be particularly important when young people are still learning the boundaries of alcohol and are vulnerable to making poor choices and the exploitation of others.

With responsibility comes independence

All of the things above can sound quite boring to adults, but they can be a genuine pleasure to their young people as they learn and develop new life skills and coping mechanisms, becoming more responsible and empowered as they grow older, and particularly pleasurable if they have been used to you doing everything for them for years. This does not always mean they will embrace change wholeheartedly to start with, but they should, eventually, enjoy the sense of independence that taking responsibility for their own health and well-being brings. Encourage them to have a sense of pride in new experiences that they have managed for themselves.

ISSUES OF HEALTH, WELL-BEING AND SAFETY FOR YOU

Major life changes create upheaval and difficulty as well as presenting challenges for development, growth and new beginnings. When children become adults and go off to study or to start their own independent living, parents are faced with probably the greatest challenge to their personal living style that they have had to deal with since their first child was born. One of the things that can make this change even more difficult is the time of life at which this tends to happen. Both men and women can find themselves at a time when career is no longer their main driving force, and considerations about when to retire are starting to crop up. Parents may also be experiencing the symptoms – and effects – of the menopause, with all the emotional and psychological disruption that this can bring. With this background, feeling sad and rudderless after many years spent gearing everything around the needs and responsibilities of the family can bring further disorientation.

It is only natural at a time of change, particularly when that change was not of our making, to reassess life and what is important. Yet when children have just left home, or are about to do so, it can be difficult to find anything compelling, exciting and important enough to make life feel good. If life feels grey and the future feels bleak, if all the good times seem to be in the past, don't worry. Take time, relax, look after yourself and in time you will almost certainly begin to feel better; particularly if you can start some new things and meet some new people along the way.

For men it can be just as unsettling as for women to see their child leave and go off into a bright new future while they themselves may be feeling tired and jaded having spent a large proportion of their lives working hard at something that can clearly go on without them when the time comes. It's no wonder that around this time so many men buy that motorbike or sports car they have always secretly longed for, or go into a time-reversal stage where they try to recapture the excitement and energy of youth.

The menopause

It is surprising how little most women are prepared for the menopause, even though it is a major contributor to women's mental and physical health issues in middle life. Understanding the emotional and physical changes that may occur would help many women appreciate what is happening as a biological process and to seek support if it is needed – rather than feeling helpless. The most widely known effect is probably the hot flushes, but there are a range of other associated symptoms, some short and others long term.

- Sudden sweats.

- Inability to sleep.

- Physical discomfort.

- Bladder weakness or irritability.

- General weariness.

- Joint pain.

Of course, there are many other medical outcomes, some of which can be far reaching such as osteoporosis and heart disease, to which women are more prone post-menopause, because the female sex hormones offer some protection during the fertile years. It is always advisable for women to have regular check-ups with their doctor and to discuss menopause symptoms and their management. Hormone replacement therapy is available and can be effective, but is not possible (or desirable) for all.

Many women experience few physical symptoms at the onset of the menopause but may begin to experience more as time passes, others may have no ill effects whatsoever and feel a sense of relief at not having to bother with periods and contraception any more; however, the statistics indicate that depression is common, with three times more women being diagnosed in their fifties than at any other time.

Underlying all the monitoring and management of symptoms there may be a profound sadness that comes with an awareness that your fertile, child-bearing days are over and that you are getting older. It is perhaps a sign of our society that age is seen negatively; in many cultures and in earlier times age was seen as the bringer of wisdom and spiritual awareness and older women in particular were revered and consulted within their communities.

Self-help

Exercise is one of the best ways to counteract the effects of the menopause. You will feel better afterwards, sleep better, have a rush of 'feel good' chemicals and perhaps meet some new people in the process.

Herbal help Many women feel they benefit from a range of herbal medicines and preparations available from chemists and supermarkets or online, such as evening primrose oil or black cohosh. The medical evidence of their value is less well established, however.

Avoid spicy food, alcohol and stimulants, such as caffeine, as these can induce hot flushes if you are susceptible.

Eat food containing soya or drink soya milk. Soya is particularly high in plant oestrogens, which some believe may help lessen menopausal symptoms.

A short course of antidepressants may help if you are experiencing profound depression, and you should talk to your doctor if you feel this would be of assistance, but remember that they do not provide a solution to any underlying issues or problems. Many GPs will be able to offer guidance on the best ways of managing a period of depression without using medication. Taking extra exercise and someone trusted to talk to might be helpful too.

Take vitamin and mineral supplements such as vitamin E, calcium and vitamin B6 if you feel your diet is lacking, but make sure you do your research first, as it is possible to overdose and cause harm by taking too much of some vitamins.

Take up some form of relaxation such as yoga or t'ai chi, both of which are also excellent for maintaining and developing flexibility. Some people find massage, flotation, aromatherapy, acupuncture and reflexology to be helpful, and certainly exploring the options can be fun.

Share your difficulties with friends, particularly if they are going through similar things themselves. It's good to know you are not alone.

You could also consider some form of counselling or psychotherapy. If you are new to therapy, it is always best to seek advice on finding the best service available. The British Association of Counselling and Psychotherapy (BACP) provides information and a comprehensive list of services and therapists in all areas.[14]

If you lack motivation consider seeking the help of a life coach.[15]

How to recognise depression

People who are generally cheerful and successful may notice depression quickly if it occurs, but for others it may be less easy to spot if they are inclined to dwell on bad news. Feeling run down and having constipation may be the symptoms of depression rather than just part of everyday life. For some, depression can feel as if they are going mad, for others it is like living in a grey, sad world from which all the joy has been sucked. The list of symptoms below is just for guidance. Many who are experiencing depression in themselves or others will recognise items on the list, but depression can be a short-term event or a much longer-term problem.

Signs of depression

There are numerous lists and symptom checkers online, but the most frequently listed symptoms include:

- Persistent sad, anxious, numb, or empty feelings.

- Feelings of worthlessness, helplessness, excessive guilt.

- Feelings of hopelessness, pessimism.

- Loss of interest or pleasure in activities that you once found enjoyable, including sex.

- Insomnia, early-morning wakefulness, or excessive sleeping.

- Decreased energy, fatigue, feeling slow or sluggish.

- Increased appetite with weight gain; decreased appetite with weight loss.

- Thoughts of self-injury or suicide, or attempting to injure yourself.

- Restlessness, irritability, nervousness.

- Diminished ability to concentrate, difficulty remembering details, or making decisions.

- Persistent physical symptoms that do not respond to treatment, such as headaches, backaches, cramps, or digestive problems.

Getting help

People suffering from depression may shy away from the thought of counselling or psychotherapy for a number of reasons. One of the most common is that they feel they should be able to manage their lives without help and support, whereas in reality we all need help and support, particularly at the more difficult times of our lives, and learning to accept support is a valuable life lesson at any age, as it enables us to be better at giving it too. Therapy may also be rejected for financial reasons, and while this may be a valid consideration, being honest about how much we spend on things to make us feel better (shopping, alcohol, chocolate) could help us view counselling not as an expense but as a saving. Counselling can also be seen as an education process for life – an investment in a healthy future.

It is possible to get counselling through the health service, although waiting lists can be long and places limited, and some areas operate charity-based services with reduced rates for those on a limited income. It's worth exploring what's available locally – you might even find individual therapists who are willing to reduce their fees, particularly for short-term support.

The other important factor to remember when embarking on any course of change is that it will have a knock-on effect on those closest to us, including partners and children. Family and friends may be resistant to those they live with entering therapy, because they will understand that they will most likely be talked about. Most relationships are based on give and take, although not always fairly, and anything that changes this balance may change a relationship dramatically. Although for those entering therapy, change may be a desired outcome, for their partners this can be threatening and they may be unsupportive or hostile. Where finances are shared, negotiating access to funding something that is not agreed to by both parties may impact on an individual's ability to commit.

Other issues of health and safety

Avoiding habits that are dangerous for you Think back over the last ten years and give yourself an honest appraisal. Have any of the following increased significantly in the time period?

- Alcohol consumption?

- Gambling, including bingo or online gambling, playing the lottery?

- Eating?

- Smoking?

- Taking painkillers?

- Working, and in particular, bringing work home to complete?

- Obsessive interests or viewpoints such as the state of the world, politics, the cost of living?

- Obsessive emailing, texting, social networking sites or phone calls – particularly late at night?

- Talking about problems all the time to a range of different people to garner a range of opinions and thoughts?

- Computer games or puzzles?

If any of the above have increased significantly in the last year then you may need some help. Gradual increases sometimes happen without us even noticing until we stop and take stock, but a sudden and dramatic increase that has been sustained for some time can become entrenched and begin a life-long struggle to change unless we recognise what we are doing and get appropriate help early on.

Depriving yourself of habits that are good for you Check back over the last ten years again – have any of these decreased significantly?

- Sleep?

- Spending easy and relaxed time with friends?

- Time spent on hobbies and interests?

- Regular exercise?

- Reading for pleasure?

Have a look at your answers, and be honest with yourself. What do they tell you? Only you can know what you need in your life, and only you can begin to make the small changes necessary to improve your health and well-being over time.

Singles safety

For the single, or newly single, parent it is often only when the children leave home that parents feel free to explore close personal or sexual relationships again.

Using dating sites

By far the most popular way of finding potential partners is to use an Internet dating site because it offers anonymity and ease of access to information. There is a wealth of sites, some free and others with differing rates of financial commitment. Take time to browse, talk to friends about sites they have used and what they like, and don't sign any contract or give any banking details until you have done your homework. Observe before you commit, and if in doubt don't do it.

Reputable dating sites offer sound guidance to their users on safety, so make sure you read it and follow it. Key rules to follow include:

- Don't give any personal details like your address or full name – you may even prefer to use a site that provides a mail box rather than one which expects you to give your own email address.

- Don't give out personal information, such as children's names or your place of work.

- If meeting someone, make sure someone knows where you are going, meet in a public place, leave your mobile phone on and plan your transport home in advance.

- Never put your children's ages on your profile. There is evidence that paedophiles trawl through such sites to find targets and then approach parents as prospective partners.

- If meeting someone doesn't go well, don't be afraid to leave.

- Make the first meeting short – perhaps lunch rather than dinner.

Long-distance relationships

Such sites can introduce potential partners who are from overseas or who live a long way from home. Many of these relationships are genuine, but some are entered into for financial gain by playing on the needy, gullible or naive. Be aware that if anyone asks you for money or mentions difficulties they are having that could be resolved by money (such as, my sister is very sick and needs an operation, but I can't afford it) or offers to visit if cash is forthcoming, be very wary. Accept only if you are prepared to lose your money. There is a huge industry, mostly now Internet based, in mail-order partners with agencies offering introduction services to partners, usually women, from a variety of countries. Most of these women are trying to start a new life in Britain and are willing to marry to do so. There is no reason why such a marriage cannot be fulfilling; many arranged marriages are happy and last a lifetime, no matter how strange they may seem to those more used to a romantic view of relationships, but keep your feet on the ground and make sure that you enter any such relationship with legal advice. Choose a partner who is looking for a family and lifetime commitment rather than one whom you find only physically attractive and who may not share your life goals.

Sexually transmitted infections (STIs)

The strong increase reported by doctors in the number of people in their forties and fifties presenting with sexually transmitted infection is probably due to the 'dating frenzy' many newly single parents experience when they try to socialise more. This is partly due to their inexperience and reluctance with condoms, which were used solely for contraception in their youth but now have a major role to play in preventing diseases and infections such as HIV and chlamydia that were not prevalent 25 years ago. Older singles, especially those who have had the same sexual partner for a long period of time or most of their sexual life, have not had to adjust to the changes in sexual-health behaviour now required.

Asking new partners about their sexual history, although a sensible precaution, may not provide you with any realistic information on which to judge their health, partly because people lie, and partly because infection can occur through any sexual contact, not just to the promiscuous, and carrying a sexually transmitted infection may produce no symptoms, meaning the individual is unaware. All sexually active adults should regularly have check-ups at a sexual-health centre, if there is any chance that they could have contracted an infection but also to ensure other health issues are being monitored, such as prostate or cervical cancer.

Many men do not like using condoms, particularly if they are not used to using them, but it is a sensible precaution and a wise habit to get into. For most women, using condoms is no different from not using them, but for older women they may increase dryness, so extra lubrication is recommended. Most big supermarkets now sell condoms, lubricants and a variety of other sexual-health purchases, and be aware that a non-latex condom is available for anyone with a sensitivity to rubber. If a partner will not use a condom, then perhaps you should reconsider them as a sexual partner, and find someone who is both more in tune with your needs and more willing to take care to protect you from harm.

QUESTIONS AND ANSWERS

Q: 'I have not had sex with anyone but my husband for a very long time. After my marriage broke up I did eventually start dating, but I feel unable to ask someone to use a condom. It really worries me. I feel out of touch and unable to insist.'
A: Many people find talking about sex difficult, and if you haven't had to negotiate sex for a long time you are bound to find it difficult or embarrassing. But the person you will be talking to will almost certainly be able to empathise with that difficulty. If they don't, perhaps this relationship is not going to be one in which you can fully express yourself.

You could use 'Questions' on Yahoo, pose a question anonymously and see what people say.[16] This gets you used to talking about sex and using the vocabulary – hearing it come out of your mouth cold can feel odd. Perhaps you have a friend who is more comfortable and you can discuss issues without being made to feel naive and out of touch. Perhaps you know someone in a similar situation who had a partner but has since moved on and had other relationships. You need to build up the confidence to say that using a condom is a condition of the relationship going further and is in both your interests. If you can't say it – email it or text it. Simple is always best – if you are arranging a first night together simply ask him to make sure he brings condoms, if it happens more spontaneously at your place, simply say, 'I have condoms.' He'll get the message.

Q: 'When it comes to drinking, how much is too much? My daughter goes out and gets sloshed every weekend. I'm aware of the government's recommended guidelines, but she is only young once and I'm worried that if I am too heavy handed she may stop talking to me altogether.'

A: Spotting when it is getting out of hand is important, and if every weekend is a party, and if she's drinking to get drunk every week, then it's too much. You should be aware of the long-term effects of binge drinking, and as a responsible parent, discuss this with your daughter. She risks getting into a pattern where there is a real danger of feeling unable to have fun without alcohol, and this can lead to life-long problems and addiction. In the short term, she is also putting herself at risk of becoming involved in fights or violence, pregnancy, STIs and getting into dangerous situations. Surely all this is worth the risk of her being cross with you? You are her parent, after all, not her friend. Interestingly, parental disapproval is one of the things that may help a young person restrict their alcohol intake – an appreciation that 'My mum will kill me if I go home drunk again this week!' may deter.

You also need to have a serious talk with her, perhaps questioning what is fun. Does she feel more herself with drink inside her? If you don't want to seem preachy, use press coverage and television storylines from soap operas to promote discussion.

Q: 'My daughter is planning to hitchhike to Morocco over Easter and I'm worried. It is an organised scheme, run by a charity, but it feels irresponsible to be encouraging them to do this.'

A: Check out the information the organisers and your daughter can provide for parents and their inevitable concerns. Make a list of all your worries and questions in detail and talk them through with your daughter and her friends – the worst that will happen is that they think you are overly hung up on danger – and you can live with that.

Reassure yourself on the structure of the groups hitching together, how they identify themselves, perhaps through T-shirts, and the advice and support they have been given through the charity for which they are raising money. If the charity is unaware of the event, they should be notified – it is in their name, after all. Make sure the groups understand how important following simple safety rules are, such as staying together and making notes of car numbers – perhaps having a 'text buddy' back home or within the charity who they keep in text contact with when getting new lifts.

Alison was in just this position and found it was a life-enhancing experience for her daughter that put the young people in situations where decisions had to be made. They realised they had skills and competencies they had forgotten about or didn't recognise previously, such as map reading and making themselves understood in French. Like Alison, you may end up being very proud of your child.

CHAPTER 7

Sofa Syndrome

What is sofa syndrome? Most of us will grasp its meaning, even if it's just a dim memory from the days BC (before children). As an adult, it's often an indulgence; as a young person, it can be a regular occurrence – and for some it's a problem.

ENCOURAGING YOUR YOUNG PERSON TO BE ACTIVE

What we are calling sofa syndrome is that spiral of boredom, low motivation and low energy that comes from having nothing meaningful to do with your time. In a busy life, it's generally a pleasure to have a few hours with the phone switched off, the door closed and something to watch or read that requires little effort. But, like all pleasures, carried to the extreme it can become addictive and unhealthy if an occasional pleasure becomes a daily occurrence.

For some young people life can become permanent downtime, and they may spend their waking hours flopped in front of the TV, making occasional trips to the kitchen for instant food and snacks – with only occasional breaks in the routine.

Many young people lead busy and active lives, even within the parameters of limited finances and fewer choices than their parents. They spend time with friends, they play sports, they go to new places to explore, they network and organise their time, they invent and develop schemes and ideas, and they hardly ever sit still. For every young person there will be the odd day when all they want to do is chill in comfort, and providing they are not avoiding obligations by doing so, there is no harm in this.

There are other young people, however, who cannot think of any meaningful way of using their time without spending money, so when there is no money they do nothing. If they are then unable to find work, their sense of personal worth diminishes, and along with it their ability to motivate themselves. Within their peer group many young people place a lot of emphasis on material possessions, such as designer clothing or the 'right' mobile phone – visible signs of cash flow and evidence of their popularity (such as the number of friends on Facebook). If these are the things that matter to a young person, having no job is a far greater handicap than it might be to a young person with different values, one who believes that it is the person you are and the effort and intention you put into life that make a difference. Before we criticise value systems based purely on material possessions and evidence of popularity, perhaps we should question the influences they are picking up – from their family and wider society – about what is important in life.

How to tell if there is a problem

Young people are naturally pretty energetic most of the time, but all young people have times when their energy levels crash. If they have had several late nights on the trot and not been getting enough sleep, they may seem particularly tired. But whereas young people need more sleep than adults, many probably get considerably less, largely because their world is new and exciting, and sleep seems such a waste of time. The need to catch up on sleep also seems to develop with age, so a 16-year-old may spend half the weekend coming back to life whereas a 20-year-old may only need to catch up after a particularly hectic time.

How do you spot sofa syndrome?

Whereas all young people may need the occasional catch-up on sleep, and the list that follows may apply to many young people on a regular basis, it's important to bear in mind that general lack of motivation may imply depression or evidence of a wider problem. And there may be causes other than lack of sleep. Losing a job, not getting accepted at one's first choice place of higher education and being dumped by a girlfriend or boyfriend can throw anyone into a short-term depression, but most young people will bounce back in a matter of days. Certain items on the list below, marked with an asterisk, should always be considered as a sign that all is not well, as they imply depression linked to low self-worth and lack of motivation that are either ongoing or getting worse. In such cases their behaviour and outlook should be monitored carefully. Signs include:

- Less attention to personal hygiene than ideal – not showering, washing hair or cleaning their teeth as often as is socially acceptable.

- Lack of attention to personal appearance.

- Spending four hours or more at one go lying on a sofa, lying in/on the bed awake, sitting at a computer or console playing games or surfing the net (without making contact with anyone else).

- More than three cups or plates around the sofa or bed by the end of a day.

- Staying home without friends or social contact during weekends and evenings.

- Turning down invitations from friends.

- Not answering calls/network contacts.

- Silent and withdrawn, possibly surly or aggressive.

- Not showing any kindness or affection to others, no interest in others.

- Increase in bad habits, such as smoking more, drinking more, eating more junk, intentionally staying awake, misuse of drugs and substances.

- Intentional self-harm such as cutting or bruising themselves.*

- Expressing dislike for themselves and their life.

- Talk of suicide – even if not relating it to themselves; fascination with death.*

- Unshakeable and disproportionate belief that one thing will transform their life; for example, a surgical procedure such as plastic surgery or being slimmer, having a six-pack, having a car, getting a partner.*

- Becoming obsessive about one thing with evidence that nothing else in their life is of any importance; for example, counting calories, a particular game, a sport or team, their appearance.*

Breaking the cycle

No one likes to feel helpless, and the young person who is opting out off life by doing nothing is caught in a spiral from which they

---

* These might indicate that something is seriously wrong and may require specialist help, support and input. If you are in doubt, talk to your GP, who will be able to offer advice to you as a parent but not offer treatment to your young person through you – they would need to make their own appointment.

cannot exit. Most will have a viewpoint on what will make all the difference – perhaps a job, some money, a nice girlfriend/boyfriend, some new friends – but while they may have an image of what will break the cycle, they lack both skills and motivation to move towards change. They may daydream about winning the lottery or becoming a celebrity – two modern-day magic wands to transform their life into one of wealth and comfort without any effort on their part. Or they may have unrealistic and unobtainable views of the future, without envisaging the steps that might move them towards their goal; for example, wanting to own a chain of designer shops rather than working in one. Of course, there is nothing wrong with having ambitions, but to succeed they will need to learn about the market they wish to enter and gain skills that are likely to be useful, and if they show no motivation towards learning, either academically or practically, then they are simply daydreaming!

The role of a parent here requires patience, understanding and skill, with a fair bit of tongue biting. Repeatedly telling someone else how to live their life, when you are clearly living by different standards, is unlikely to motivate them to change – and being told they are wrong or misguided is similarly unlikely to be positively received. Even if they are looking for help, they may not make those who are criticising or judging them on a regular basis their first port of call.

CASE STUDY: JOE, 17, AND HIS MOTHER NICOLE

Joe left school at 16 with few qualifications. He was hoping to find a job involving physical, preferably outdoor, work, and in which he could progress. He is not academic and does not particularly enjoy learning, but he is a very talented footballer and all-round sportsperson, and had been a regular member of school teams and a keen participant in many after-school clubs and societies. Since leaving school he became much less active, as most of his sporting activities revolved around school, and he has never joined or been part of any other teams or groups.

Since leaving school he has had only one job, which was in a small local supermarket. He hated the routine and the mindlessness of his role, which consisted mainly of shelf stacking and loading and unloading, and as there were not many employees, and none of his age, he felt isolated and unsupported. He gradually took more and more time off work until eventually he was fired after being warned that he needed to behave more responsibly. Since losing the job without the prospect of a good reference, he has been unable to find other work and has gradually become more and more despondent. From being an affectionate, outgoing and friendly young man, he became withdrawn, sarcastic and sometimes spiteful to his younger sister. From having a wide friendship group he began to withdraw from friends and social contacts, eventually even throwing away his mobile phone.

His mother, Nicole, became increasingly concerned about his behaviour and attitude, as he became clearly more isolated and unmotivated. On a typical day, Joe would get out of bed around midday and grab a bowl of cereal and a cup of tea, which he would eat lying on the sofa in his underwear where he would remain for most of the day until Nicole and his sister, Patsy, returned from work and school. There would often be a ring of debris around the sofa, including the breakfast bowls, bread crusts, empty packets from crisps, biscuits and scattered papers, such as the fliers that come through the door, and catalogues of special offers.

His hygiene became problematic, because he would not change his clothes for several days, seldom showered without being told to, or change his bedclothes. His father, who was no longer living with the family, was very concerned for his son's state of mind and would regularly phone, firing questions at him and then pointing out all the things he should be doing and the consequences for the future of his current behaviour. Joe would frequently lock himself in his room for hours after a phone call from his father.

His mum tried to encourage him to look for work, but he felt there was no point. He had already had several rejections and began to voice his hatred for his old boss with increasing frequency, hating him for firing him and hating the world in general for not giving him what he wanted and needed. He felt everything was unfair to him. Any attempt by Nicole to get him to see that his present circumstances were not only of his own making but were in his control, led to anger outbursts followed by, on one occasion, his disappearance for three days.

After careful review, discussion and consultation, Nicole came up with a plan to support her son, which involved three stages:

1 Getting him back into the world of work, being physically active and spending time with others.
2 Improving his self-worth by helping him to recognise his strengths and achievements.
3 Helping Joe to identify what he wanted, realistically for his future and the steps that he might take to make that happen.

Nicole began by giving him small tasks to do, for which she paid him, such as cleaning the car and sorting out the garden. She then spoke to friends and neighbours to get more jobs for Joe, including babysitting, wallpaper stripping, helping to lay the foundations for a new garage, dog sitting and delivering leaflets. Although none of these was particularly well paid, it meant that Joe had some money to spend, and he started to make contact with some of his friends again for nights out. Nicole helped him put together a leaflet, which he put through the doors of local homes advertising his services, and he began to get a trickle of work. Every job that came in, no matter how small, helped him feel useful, and his mother spent time with him reflecting on how well he had achieved each task. Eventually, she helped him to write a brief customer-satisfaction questionnaire, which he gave to each person he worked for. Just looking at these helped Joe feel so much better about himself.

Nicole also found lists of local sporting groups, clubs and teams that did not require money, or only small fees, and Joe joined a local athletics club and a football team, which trained one evening a week and he played for them at the weekend.

After six months, Joe was back to his usual self and was actively participating in family events, helping around the house when he had time and managing his small business interests and social life well.

Nicole then spent time asking Joe to identify all the different jobs he had done and thinking about what he enjoyed in each of them to begin to draw up a profile of the kind of work he should be concentrating on in the future. He discovered, to his surprise, that he really enjoyed the work he had done indoors around painting and decorating, so he enrolled at a local college to do a course to help him learn the basic skills and techniques. One of his sporting contacts offered him a part-time job assisting in a high-end painting and decorating firm, which he worked at diligently and professionally while maintaining some of his odd-job work to supplement his income.

Practical tips for supporting your sofa-bound young person

Get them to reflect honestly on why they can't get a job. They will be disinclined to speak honestly if they feel you are going to judge or criticise them. No matter what they say, praise their honesty and willingness to reflect, and resist any temptation, particularly if they identify something you have told them about in the past, to point out how you were right all along. Ask them to consider the following:

- Are they over-qualified? This can be particularly hard if you live in an area of low employment, and employers may feel that a young person with good academic qualifications will be bored and therefore leave at the earliest opportunity. This could be true.

- Do they not interview well? Do they get interviews but not get job offers?

- Are they not putting the time and effort into applications? Do they send applications but never receive job offers or interviews? Are they applying for jobs for which they are qualified or have a real interest?

It is always wise to try to identify the specific issues relating to the job applications, because then your young person can draw up a plan to change or develop how they are currently presenting themselves. The process of being interviewed for a job should entitle them to some feedback on how the came across, and why they did not get the job, so it's worth ringing (or emailing, if it is easier) to ask for some. Other support is available online, from Connexions, Job Centres and university careers, and they may still be entitled to some guidance even several years after graduation when they are competing with a whole new cohort of leavers. See the Resources for more information.

Simple areas to be considered include:

How to make a CV stand out from the rest

Even if your young person doesn't have the best qualifications or work experience, there are things that they can say about themselves that will get the attention of a prospective employer. By being clear about their skills, by expanding their personal qualities, by sharing some of their interests (and the relevant skills learnt through those interests) they will give employers a much better picture of who this person is and what they are capable of.

A good CV will make an employer want to meet the person who wrote it out of curiosity, if nothing else. See the Resources section for useful information on CV preparation.

The covering letter or email

A CV is usually sent out with a covering letter or email, and your young person should make these really specific by engaging with the role they are applying for, perhaps going through all the person specifications or job responsibilities one by one and giving examples from their own life as to how they have learnt or developed the appropriate knowledge and skills.

Both CV and covering letter need to be specific for each job application, not a 'round robin' that has been sent to others as part of a scattergun approach to job hunting. In particular they need to watch out for:

- The language the organisation to which the application is being made uses when writing about itself. Ensure a job application mirrors and matches this, in tone and content.

- Use of an appropriate typeface and spacing, to ensure an application looks inviting, easy to read but businesslike.

- Evidence of collaboration, being a good team player, with meaningful examples. This is particularly effective if you can give examples from different areas of your life where you have worked well with others, such as organising a charity event at school, being part of a sports team at university, creating a study group for yourself, being a member of a family and pulling your weight, making arrangements/sorting disputes fairly with friends. Most organisations want people who will fit in and will be impressed if you can show you have problem solved in difficult situations.

- Verbs in the job advertisement that indicate the key skills required. Make sure you respond with evidence as to what you can do. When job applications for very popular positions are rejected by computer, it is because the computer has been scanned to spot applications that do not address the key skills sought, as evinced by the match between what was sought in the job advertisement and what information is supplied by the applicant. As a handy hint, ensure you reply to all the main capabilities sought.

- The importance of volunteering. Today, organisations have to justify their social responsibility, and evidence that you have taken on a role without expecting to be paid is strong proof that you can be relied upon to motivate yourself and others. Long periods of unemployment may be easier to explain to a potential employer if you have filled them with meaningful voluntary activity.

Encourage them to cut down on time-wasting or time-filling activities such as television or game playing by helping them to find other things to do (remember, nagging never works) such as sporting activities, taking part in charity events such as running or cycling, helping other people and noticing how it feels to be useful, volunteering or setting up an enterprise or a small business of their own. Being physically active and involved with others will help considerably in improving their motivation. The more depressed a person becomes the less willing they may be to get up and do something, so organise family events occasionally or invite others to come along if it helps. Consider gym membership for a birthday gift!

Expect them to fend for themselves; it is neither helpful nor constructive to allow them to wallow while you take care of their day-to-day needs, it benefits neither of you if you support their torpor. Expect them to maintain certain levels of behaviour and hygiene, and insist upon certain tasks being completed during the day while you are away (or even if you are not). They should not expect you to be providing the level of service they had when they were in full-time education or when they were young.

If they are living in your house but not contributing financially, we suggest you draw up an agreement – and part of this should be a list of tasks that are your young person's sole responsibility. This may seem harsh, but is in fact a way of helping them to become more independent and to take increasing responsibility for their part of the household. Ten to 15 hours a week is a reasonable amount of time to expect a young person to work to pay for their keep, and this could include cleaning, shopping, garden maintenance, childcare (if there are younger siblings), laundry tasks (not just their own) cooking or food preparation, pet care and special projects such as helping to decorate a room. If they have problems completing the tasks, draw up a detailed timetable with them.

Encourage them to watch family television with everyone else, not just on their own, in their own room. Isolation from the family is not helpful and will perpetuate feelings of difference and depression. Even if they seem annoyed and irritable when they are with the family, it is still better for them to be around others. Challenge any unacceptable behaviour kindly and set clear boundaries of what will not be tolerated but without criticism or judgement, so for example:

'Mark, please don't swear at your brother like that. It is not acceptable in this family. I know you are annoyed, but it is not fair to take it out on him. If you have an issue, talk it through sensibly.'

Would probably have a more positive effect than:

'Don't swear at your brother. I don't care how miserable you are, you shouldn't take it out on other people just because you're fed up with yourself. I'm getting really sick of your behaviour, you just slope around the house all day being grumpy and miserable, and making everybody else's life a misery.'

ENCOURAGING YOURSELF OFF THE SOFA

It's difficult living with an adult who is not working and unable to get a job, and who seems under-motivated and perhaps now even lazy. It's frustrating watching this. You see the potential in them, the possibilities all around them for employment or pro-activity for employment, and you can't get them to see it for themselves – or to do something about it if they can. Meanwhile, the rest of the world (or do we mean your friends' children, who seem to be doing awfully well) is secure and rushing on ahead. Does parenting bring out the innately competitive gene in parents, who all say they want children to be happy but in reality seem to want successful ones?

It is worth pausing to consider whether this concern on their behalf is rather masking concern about what we are going to do with our own lives. Perhaps this is all just displacement activity, and we should try to ensure our lives do not happen just at home. Detaching ourselves from the situation and going out a bit more may help us to be more objective, rather than just coming home to argue.

It's a good idea too to avoid co-dependency, which is, frankly, more likely with mothers and sons and a particular issue where the mother is a lone parent, whereby the son slots into a role that might more usually be taken by a partner. Sons in this position can acquire responsibilities for the associated chores and create a life pattern that is difficult to move away from. You move into a partnership of nagging wife and listening husband, even though the partner role is your son.

In this context, it is helpful to think about our own evolution, and that of our friends. Many roles in life are arrived at sideways, rather than through a logical and linear progression – volunteering, meeting someone, reading something and following it up – rather than the right job opportunity presenting itself and you then being appointed. Thinking about this within the family and immediate circle, can you spot anyone who is bringing in ideas and moving ahead, and doing interesting things; someone who might be willing to try to provide you all with some stimulation and points of access – not just pointing out how your lives are stuck? You could invite interesting friends around, get them to eat with you, share ideas. Or you could go to a stand-up comedy night, or attend a recording of a radio comedy show – anything to hear lively minds in action.

Rather than holding onto a golden dream you are in no danger of reaching, try to help yourself see your life developing in small steps. Highlight a long-term nirvana and then consider the constituent parts and how to get there. Replicate the experience in a series of short stages; for example, if you have always wanted to work in the Caribbean, think about working outside, in the sunshine, planning holidays, relaxing with friends and appreciating the experience. And see whether any biographies of those who have made it provide helpful hints on the process, such as key people met, important chances spotted and made the most of. Reading about the experience of others can be very motivating.

Finally, try to deal with your issues. When you suddenly have more time available you can end up devoting yourself to pursuits that are not healthy and do not promote your self-confidence or self-esteem. Use your dreams and aspirations as a way of filling your time. The issues are all the usual comfort-promoting behaviours, and we will give just three examples:

Television

It's so easy to end up watching too much television, even if we give ourselves permission by saying that we are watching ironically and with a critical eye. Keep a grasp on your own habits – is this becoming too much of a routine? Daytime television is seductive and the way it is presented (with a timetable) can make you feel busy, but it can lead to hours of doing nothing and a very passive, vicarious existence. Like pasta, it is filling and satisfying, but only in the short term.

What is too much television? Perhaps an over-regular habit. If you find yourself putting off going out in order to watch television, your priorities may need reassessing. Life is more important and the television should not dictate.

Alcohol

Empty-nest mothers are a recognisable risk group for drinking too much. The temptation to deal with your various issues through drink can be strong, as alcohol swallows your unhappiness and makes you feel understood. Try to divert the activity, going out to the cinema rather than spending £5 on a bottle of wine – or cooking with it instead.

Food

Binge eating is about self-abuse. But 'treating yourself', to make yourself feel better, for example by watching television and eating chocolate, may avoid the real issue that set off the behaviour and lead to new issues such as guilt and self-blame.

As with all these issues, running an established pattern or addiction requires you to give yourself permission to do it. Can you put some rules in place to combat this, because if rules are sensible, it feels bad if you break them. Take your mind off the desire by imagining how you might feel afterwards, if you go ahead. Try to understand and anticipate the guilt spiral and to break the process. Try thinking about exercise instead, which gets the endorphins going and always makes you feel better (although the gym every night can become an addiction too).

Instead, try coming up with new treats: a manicure, a new

lipstick, cheap earrings, walking or running, gym, cooking something for the first time, a magazine you don't usually buy, phoning a friend, buying a new DVD, listening to some music, watching a chat show or some daytime television for a while (if you don't normally do it).

Consider the patterns in your life. Any activity can be examined on the basis of whether or not it improves your life, and some good thinking can be set in place around this. Engage your family in helping you with this; they have observed you and your behaviour for a long time and may have some surprising insights. They might even know better than you what brings you satisfaction and purpose – and what just fills the time. The comparisons they may make with how their friends' families behave may provide particular insight!

QUESTIONS AND ANSWERS

Q: 'My son is coming home after university. We have a different approach: he is laid back and not very motivated, and I don't like his attitude. I am concerned about how things are going to be at home.'
A: You need to have a serious conversation about boundaries with him as amicably as possible, covering what he will do when home and the ground rules he will stick to. Bear in mind that he probably has misgivings too, so he may not be staying very long. He will essentially be living as a lodger, so he needs to be accorded a sense of what is required, such as making contributions in return for living at home, and you need to be strong enough to enforce it. Rather than worrying, think about what the boundaries should be and how best to explain them, so that they sound like the basis of a harmonious household rather than tyranny. And when you discuss them with him, do so in the context of being pleased to see him return.

Q: 'My daughter is depressed. She left college because she could not cope and came back home, and now she is unable to find a job. She does not say she is depressed, but I am sure she is feeling left behind, with no money, and her friends are moving on with their lives. She does not seem to have much contact with them now. She now regrets leaving college and can see the advantages of staying, but she is moping around. I suspect she does nothing while I am out at work all day. She is not disruptive, just very passive, and I want her to get on with her life.'

A: Step one is to get her active doing something – it doesn't matter what, just something. She could deliver leaflets, volunteer, go to a gym, just something to break the cycle of depression and inactivity. More activity will stimulate better thinking too. Put her in charge of occasional cooking; get her to decide what to cook and then go out and buy the ingredients. A bike is good because it stimulates exercise and needs to be looked after. Then when she is a little more active, get her to talk about the future. At the moment, in her passive state, she probably can't look far ahead, but if you can get her to identify what it is she dreams of, you are closer to working towards it in small steps.

Q: 'I think my son is stealing from me. He is at home all day and I have noticed that money has gone from my purse. Some of his possessions have disappeared too. He has no job and clearly finds having no money difficult, and I am not sure what he is spending it on – drink and drugs are an obvious worry. I fear he is drifting into bad habits and company.'

A: You should confront him. Let him know that you have noticed and suspect. Don't blame him but let him know that you are aware. This is the first step down a slippery slope towards dodgy behaviour, and it's up to him to want to change it. Can you help him make a plan of how he might get money by encouraging him to think about what he could be paid for: clearing gardens, dog walking, babysitting, putting up a notice offering to shift things in people's houses or doing limited DIY. Put an ad in the paper or a local shop offering a strong pair of hands, a willing shopper. What could he offer that someone else would be willing to pay for? He could look in charity shops for things to sell on eBay, then get started. You could offer a £20 float towards getting him up and running, just to encourage initiative. Then home in on the pride he gets from securing money through his own efforts. How we feel about ourselves is crucial, and you should reinforce him in taking the right path.

CHAPTER 8

Boomerangs

When faced with the return home of a young person their parents thought had moved out for good, they may feel a dramatic division of emotion. They may feel elated and happy to have their family once more intact, or at least their role as parents reinstated, and flattered that their young person chose to do this, but they may also feel a hint of dread that a stage in their lives that they had thought was complete is about to have an encore.

DEALING WITH THE RETURNER

Those parents who have managed to move on with their lives most successfully will probably be the ones who are most unsettled by a returning young adult. Those who were still hankering for the old days may be hanging up the bunting and icing the cake!

It's not an automatic given that any young person wishing to return to their family home is allowed to do so. You do have choices. In some instances, the return will be of short duration anyway, as your young person is simply adjusting to a life change before moving on – say after university and while looking for a job. But in other cases the young person is returning without any sense of urgency and may consider living with you simply as 'home', with no further thoughts of moving.

Being clear

In order to manage the associated changes, there are some issues that need to be addressed straightaway, and one of these is background information. A good starting point is conversation.

The biggest question of all is to ask how long they think they will be staying and what are the criteria by which they will choose to stay or leave; for example, are they waiting until they have a job? Are they waiting until they have saved enough for a deposit? Or are they just waiting until they feel ready?

Each of these reasons for wanting to return might require a different approach from you as a supportive parent, depending on whether you want them to leave or stay. You might offer to help with their savings by taking some money from them to keep, safe from temptation. You might support them in finding a job or you might help them to identify the skills and competencies they need to develop in order to live independently, and begin to teach them these.

Knowing your child as you do, their rationale will also give you a clearer timeline. If your child likes to buy lots of clothes, go out with friends every night, have foreign holidays and the latest phone, if they are staying with you until they can afford to leave, you can probably anticipate a long stay. If, on the other hand, they are regrouping their assets with the next stage of their career in mind, they are likely to be focused on coming home as a short-term stage.

Some other things to be clear about:

- **Rent** If your young person is coming to stay with you, and earning, it is not unreasonable for them to contribute to the costs of running the house.

- **What is and what is not included in the rent?** For example, food, utilities, broadband connection and fees, lifts, use and running costs of the car.

- **Bringing friends back and who can stay over** – where they sleep, when you are notified/asked, how many at any one time.

- **Friends** and the hours at which they can drop by or ring up.

- **Couch surfing**[17] and other inroads into your home Can friends/acquaintances stay when your young person is not there?

- **Key** Who has a key?

- **Safety and security** Checking procedures at home before going out or going to bed.

- **Behaviour at home** The way of speaking, not monopolising the television, kitchen or bathroom.

- **Standards of cleanliness** in own room.

- **Willingness to clean up communal areas** to agreed schedules (when the washing-up gets done, before or after a meal, can be particularly irritating).

- **Subtenants**

- **Time and money contribution** to their upkeep. They may expect the continuation of allowances that you gave during student years, particularly if they are not working full-time.

- **Decorating** and hanging up pictures in their room.

- **Use of candles** etc. (wax in the carpet and safety risk).

- **Mess** in their room. Is it allowed or not?

Being fair

If you were about to share your home with a lodger you would probably take great care to establish guidelines and ground rules, and to treat him or her respectfully and fairly (while hoping they will do the same for you). When sharing your home with your own returning young adult, ideally the same should apply.

In reality, and given the shared history between you, with much of it based on them when they were considerably younger and less mature, it can be hard to be formal about arrangements. Most parents treat their adult children differently from other adults, and not just because the bond is closer or tighter, but also because when they look at the adult they still see the child. Treating a young adult as an equal at all times may mean surrendering a lot of your hard-won parent power, especially as they may not always respond as an adult themselves – they are, after all, still learning. When in doubt, ask yourself: if this were someone else's child who was living in your house, how you would deal with the situation?

It is often easier to do things yourself, or to put up with them, than to talk them through and negotiate a fair solution – but unmanaged resentments can so easily fuel big problems later on. When a young person leaves, their parents are liberated from the silent resentment of what they once put up with in order to keep the peace, and they have become used to not being annoyed by inconsiderate behaviour. It follows that the return of the young person and their previously unaddressed behaviours can irritate those they left behind. Just as the two parties begin living together again, you have silent resentment on the one hand and lack of awareness of the problems on the other. It's not a foundation for harmonious living arrangements, and it's important for both parties to learn to negotiate unemotionally.

'When I have to talk to them about something like leaving washing-up all over the kitchen or towels in a wet heap in the bathroom, the usual kinds of things that have caused friction for years, I simply imagine I am at work talking to a work colleague. I find this allows me to detach from all the hundreds of times when I have said the same things over the years. When I talk to a colleague I expect them to respect our shared space, so it is easy to simply request a change. That way I find I don't bring up last week or last year, nor do I get cross. I've also found that if I make a clear and simple request, my daughter usually takes it on board without a fuss.' **Jess, mother of 21-year-old Lucy and 19-year-old Cameron.**

In the interest of fairness, it is also important to ask yourself whether what you are making a point about is really important or simply a matter of differing viewpoints and standards. If you are truly committed to being two or three adults sharing a space, and your young person is contributing to the budget, there may be times when you simply have to change the way you do things, to let go of control and work on your ability to tolerate and share.

'When my son first came back from university I found it very difficult. We had got used as a family to doing things in certain ways and he burst in like a tornado! Guy is messy, slapdash and full of boundless energy – all of which are admirable at some level, but very different from me. As a busy working mum, I have always endeavoured to have the house running like clockwork, and suddenly he was this whirling dervish in our midst, and I was struggling with the old impulses to criticise and control, and my desire to create a sympathetic environment for all of us. After a great deal of talking, negotiating, setting rules and boundaries, I realised that the person who needed to change was me. It really doesn't matter if there are books left on the dining table, washing-up in the sink as long as they are cleared away by the next time I need to use the table or kitchen. I'm not finding it easy, I hadn't realised how controlling I was until now, but I'm accepting that we both have rights and he has the right to be the way he is too.' **Janette, mother of 22-year-old Guy**

Becoming sharers

For many parents, the idea of becoming a house or flat sharer again is not appealing. Although many will have enjoyed the experience when they were young, everybody who did share will have some stories of nightmare housemates and difficult situations. It is part of becoming a mature adult that you create your own environment, and your own way in which to live.

To live with your returning young person as an equal requires a huge shift for many parents. The course of their life has taught them that the way in which they live is perhaps the best, or even the only, way to live. After 20 or 30 years of doing it 'my way', learning to allow things to change can be hard, which is why so many parents simply maintain the old roles of me = Mum/Dad, and you = child. Of course, this is a choice and many make it. We meet many parents who still cook, clean and iron for their young people and want nothing more than to be considered a great mum/dad or that bizarre accolade 'my best friend'. Many parents and children will say that their relationship is more like that of siblings or friends, and if this is true, then this is quite remarkable. In most relationships where this is said however, it is the case that the parent is maintaining both the majority of the workload and the responsibility.

In many ways, a good relationship between a parent and child is far more than any friendship could ever be – so perhaps we should start by reclaiming its true nature rather than simply downgrading the relationship to that of a friend. The role of a friend is to stroke, comfort, support and have fun together, and although the role of a parent may be all of these, there is also a role in challenging, leading and supporting behaviour rather than always agreeing with their child. For a child, a parent is the person you can try out all sorts of behaviours with, secure in the knowledge that they have your best interests at heart and will never get fed up and walk away. Friends tend not to be quite so tolerant.

Even when they are in their twenties, your offspring are still your children and you are still their parent. This is a relationship that has a huge history and comes with an emotional tie unlike any other relationship. Honouring this on both sides will be the biggest support to creating change within your relationship.

TALKING ABOUT PROBLEMS

There are bound to be many frustrations in your new relationship, and finding appropriate ways to talk about issues when they arise may take some time, particularly if your joint history of communication has not been good up until now.

Something that is important to recognise is that young people frequently resent any attempt to 'boss them' or tell them what to do – although, let's face it, none of us likes it very much – and they may respond with anger/fault-finding directed at you or anyone/anything less able to stick up for themselves, as well as sulking and avoidance. None of this is helpful and may result in everyone feeling disinclined to address any issues for fear of the consequences.

There are simple ways round this by letting go of your position of always being right and in charge, and by taking up one of being equal and asking for help to make improvements. We do this by behaving in a more assertive way, which means that whenever possible you simply ask for a change in behaviour and phrase it as a request, so:

> 'For goodness sake! You're 22 – can't you pick up the towels when you've finished? Do you have to leave them all over the floor for me to pick up? Honestly, you are the most selfish person I've ever met!'

Will be more likely to create an argument or residual bad feeling than:

'Please leave the bathroom tidy when you have finished.'

If you have asked for a change more than once and it still isn't happening, they need to understand why you are asking. This does not mean telling them all your thoughts and opinions around the issue or your frustrations at having to ask more than once, simply your reasons:

'I find it annoying when I try to fill the kettle in the sink and I cannot fit it under the tap because of all the washing-up in there.'

If there is still no change in their behaviour, it is necessary to have a proper discussion requiring eye contact and probably sitting down! They need to understand that they are living with you as a reciprocal relationship, and not as a given right. Not that most parents would dream of evicting their young adult, but that young adult needs to realise that they have to change their attitude to their home. It is no longer their right but their privilege to live there with you.

It might be helpful to consider the three key ways of responding according to assertion techniques:

The passive response Put up with it if needs be; sort it out yourself.

PLUS POINTS No arguments, no recriminations.

NEGATIVE POINTS Nothing changes and a precedent is set.

The aggressive response Tell them what you think of them, pull rank, insist that it's your way or no way, threaten.

PLUS POINTS You may get your way, and they may be intimidated into changing their behaviour.

NEGATIVE POINTS Resentment is created and may emerge later. Using power in the relationship will not encourage honesty or equality, someone will feel unfairly treated, one person will be infantilised or treated like a child and may respond by behaving like one.

The assertive response Telling them how you feel and requesting a change of behaviour without blame and in a reasonable and equal manner.

PLUS POINTS They can hear and understand what is being said, as it is clear and will be able to respond in an adult manner (although they may choose not to).

NEGATIVE POINTS It may not come naturally to you!

There is one other way of responding, which is really a combination of two of the above, and that is a passive–aggressive response.

The passive–aggressive response Make snide comments, make 'jokes' about the things you are unhappy with, moan to everyone else about their behaviour but not to them, make belittling comments in front of their friends, use spiteful gestures, such as deliberately unplugging their phone charger.

PLUS POINTS This is the revenge category, so may be appealing on the grounds that they are causing unhappiness so they should experience some.

NEGATIVE POINTS Nobody feels good and nobody wins. Spiteful behaviour can escalate on both sides.

Of course, written down this all sounds wonderfully simple, but for many people, being assertive about their needs and wants is not straightforward at all. Often they find they need to quote some form of authority ('your mother/father would be shocked ... ') to prove they are in the right or insist on strongly accepted social norms ('the person who uses the last piece of loo paper is supposed to replace the roll'). Alternatively, they may rely on extending the argument ('I've been on my feet all day, I've still got a whole load of ironing to do and the least you could do is take your own plates to the dishwasher'). Being assertive means being able to stick up for your own rights as well as honouring the rights of others – being neither the martyr nor the saint!

If you have allowed your child to get away with things from an early age, or if you are one of those people who thinks it is easier to do things yourself than explain or argue about them, you may need to enlist some help from friends and family when it comes to setting clear boundaries and expressing them assertively. Your young person should not be doing any less than you in terms of household chores or household management. By the time they are a young adult, all responsibilities should be shared equally, and it is probably up to the older adults to make the changes happen.

Remember, you have a right to:

- **Privacy** Both private space and private time.

- **Peace of mind** Honest dealings in relation to whereabouts and timings.

- **Equal use of shared equipment, living spaces and possessions** TV, computer, hairdryer, bathroom, and so on.

- **Your personal possessions** These should never be used without your express permission (not 'well, you said I could use it last time').

- **Equal division of chores** and household tasks between all adult family members with smaller divisions for under-16s, according to age.

- **Be taken care of** when you are unwell or experiencing difficulty for any reason.

- **Be respected** and listened to.

- **Contribute to all decisions** where the outcome has some effect on you – not just about the largest number of people wanting one thing being able to 'win'. If you have three football-mad sons who watch TV with their dad in the living room every Saturday, you have just as much right to NOT have the TV on as they do to have it on. The situation needs a compromise, such as they can watch it at home every other week and some-where else on alternate weeks, and so on.

- **Be lazy sometimes**, as well as being wrong, grumpy, mean, sad or selfish. It may not be nice, but letting everyone else be all these things without giving in to them too can be very hard work.

QUESTIONS AND ANSWERS

Q: 'My son's girlfriend is always at our house. I like her, but she is virtually living there and that's not what we agreed when he came home to live.'

A: I suggest you sit down with your son and talk to him. See how serious he is about the relationship (that's why it's a good idea to talk to him first, on his own) and discuss how you are finding the situation that she is always there. If this is a relationship to which they are both committed, you could consider negotiating her per-manent presence, but this should be accompanied by some negotiated financial and physical boundaries (rent, responsibili-ties, agreed contributions in kind) rather than just happening without anyone noticing that such a big change has taken place.

If you already know that you don't want her moving in per-manently, then you need to make that clear.

Q: 'Whose responsibility is the garden? My daughter says she does not use it, so why should she help with the upkeep? She refuses to assist. Is this reasonable?'

A: The garden is part of the property, and if you live in a property you have a responsibility for it all, not just the parts you use most frequently, in the same way that you would not neglect to lock the front door even though you do not spend much time in the hall. Living at home on a low (or no) rent is a privilege, not a right, and she could find somewhere much less convenient to stay. I would take a firm line on this and insist she helps, although perhaps allocate a specific task to her so that she knows precisely what her responsibilities are and can even begin to take pride in managing them well.

Q: 'My son and his girlfriend make a huge amount of noise in their room – much of which the rest of the house have little choice but to endure. We find it particularly embarrassing when we can hear them having sex. But they have nowhere else to go, and it would be embarrassing to raise this with them.'

A: If they are living in a shared house, they have a responsibility to consider the rights of others who share the space. Try to talk to your son on his own and explain how others feel when hearing their antics. As alternatives, they could try to use the space when others are not around, play music to hide the sounds (provided it's not late at night) or just use more discretion. Although tackling the discussion of something you find embarrassing is tricky (particularly if they don't appear to feel the same), the situation sounds difficult at the moment, so if you don't want this to become the norm, you do need to say something. Concentrate on how you all feel when you hear what you hear, not on describing the noise they are making.

Q: 'Whenever I want to wear my designer belt I have to start my search in my daughter's room. I never see her wear it, but it's always there. What should I do? In a sense, it's quite flattering that she likes something I own enough to want to borrow it.'

A: Harmonious living with other people requires the respecting of boundaries. If the constant re-housing of your belt is inconveniencing you, then you should make it clear that property is owned, and if she has not got your permission, then she shouldn't take it. Asking permission requires planning. The common response of 'you were not here to ask' is not good enough.

CHAPTER 9

Hotel Mum and Dad

One of the oldest and most widely used criticisms of a young person by their parents must surely be, 'You use this place like a hotel!'

Our parents said it to us, our friends' parents said it to them and we all at some time say it to our own children. And, as more and more young people continue to live at home well into their twenties, it is an accusation likely to live on.

BEING TAKEN FOR GRANTED
BY YOUR YOUNG PERSON

Of course, there is a great appeal in a hotel in that it is a serviced environment where towels dropped on the floor are magically picked up and swapped with clean ones, meals can be ordered at any time of the day or night, everything is cleaned and tidied once a day without ever having to see the person doing it, and when you feel like a little privacy you can hang a little tag on the door that says 'Do not disturb'. The other great appeal about living in a hotel is that you can walk in and out whenever you choose, without asking anyone's permission, announcing where you are going – or answering questions about your choices.

It is not surprising, then, that young people choose to behave as if they would like to live in a hotel environment. After all, many of the services of a hotel have been provided for them all through their lives, although perhaps the freedoms have not always been there. The challenge for parents is to help them realise that life has moved on from when everything was provided and done for them when, from a young person's point of view, they can see no benefit whatsoever in changing. Losing all their services, and having to do everything for themselves is not appealing, and will probably not be embraced willingly.

They may also need to learn that being part of a family involves more than just history and geography, it requires interaction, commitment, care and mutual support for all family members. To many young people, their family is simply their base, a place to move out from, and they give little thought to the place or responsibility within that unit, because they have never had to. As a child, the adults take responsibility for maintaining and managing the family and its interactions with each other to such an extent that to their child it may seem that no effort is being made at all – it is an automatic process. The negotiation, encouragement, care and crisis management that many parents undertake in order to put the physical and emotional needs of their children first may be so well managed that ironically it is all but invisible.

Your young person may, of course, have noticed every time something has turned out badly and they will very probably consider that to be the fault of their parent. Young people moving towards independent living frequently give very little thought to their parents' needs and wishes – probably because they have never learnt to, and perhaps because this has never been encouraged or expected.

When children were younger, the ongoing bargaining point for parents was the growing young person's desire for freedom, but by the time they are young adults, it is no longer appropriate to restrict their coming and going in this way. If you have read our previous book, *Whatever! A Down-to-earth Guide to Parenting Teenagers*, you may remember the art of balancing increasing responsibility with increasing freedom, but if you have not got into the habit of negotiating with each other, you may find you have little left that your young person values enough to bargain with.

The challenge for parents, then, is how far they are willing to allow their home and their living circumstances to change during the process of realignment. If mum and dad stop picking up the towels, it may take a long time before their adult child does it for themselves – so how long are you willing to live with wet towels on the floor? Most parents would like their child to be more responsible and to take responsibility for themselves and their actions at home. They would like them to look after themselves and to take a shared role in all household chores and tasks. But although they say they want their young person to change, mothers in particular are notoriously bad at withdrawing their labour to precipitate change in their young adult children. To be fair, let's be clear about our own motivation. If you didn't have to do it, and someone else was happy to do it for you, would you still:

- Do the ironing?

- Clean the car?

- Load and unload the dishwasher?

- Make the beds?

- Clean and tidy the house?

- Wash the kitchen floor?

- Clean the bathroom?

- Do the laundry?

Perhaps a useful starting point is to show this list to your young adult and ask them which of these chores they have done lately – or even done at all. Many young people, when confronted with such a list, are horrified that anyone would expect them to do these jobs, and we have met several young people who have adamantly refused even to consider doing any kind of domestic chore under any circumstances. If this is the case in your home, you have only yourself to blame!

There is only one rule if you want your child to be more responsible: you need to stop doing everything for them and start to expect them to do it for themselves. It's a hard truth, and it is not without repercussions for the parents, as everyone in the family will have to change their lifestyle, and possibly status, along with it. When everyone takes responsibility for themselves within the family, they become, more than ever, a group of equal adults sharing a living space.

Will they stay or will they go?

If parents are ambivalent about having their young adult children still living at home, it may be for a variety of reasons. On the one hand they feel flattered that their child still wants to be with them and sympathetic with their situation of being unable to afford a home of their own, and yet on the other hand they may long for a more peaceful life than is possible with a young adult in the house. However, as we have discussed, having them leave is an enormous jolt to any parent, and one which most people put off for as long as possible. This may be one of the reasons why parents continue to treat their young adult as a child by looking after them, so they are unintentionally ensuring that their child is not able to fully function out in the real world. This would seem to be particularly true with boys who, even in our modern, enlightened times, are still not expected to deal with domestic chores fully by many parents.

Some young people may tell their parents that they will leave, and even use it as a threat every time they are asked to do something they don't like or if they are expected to behave in a mature and sensible way. A wise parent will simply ignore the bluster, but a scared parent may well appease and avoid confrontation by not expecting their young adult to contribute in any way they are unwilling to. The truth is that most young people living at home are there because they want to be, although their reasons can be varied and may include money, geography, familiarity, fear of the unknown or simply a desire to be still living in a supportive and loving environment.

In the end they will go – they are meant to, and it would be a sad waste if they didn't. Although a 23-year-old still living at home might be a cause for congratulations – 'What wonderful parents you are that your child still wants to live with you' – a 45-year-old still living at home is quite another matter – 'What awful parents they are to make their child so dependent and guilty that he/she feels the need to stay and look after them.'

The time to leave is when they have the basic skills for self-management, and these can be very basic indeed, such as:

- Keeping him- or herself clean – and that includes buying and using relevant toiletries.

- Keeping their clothes clean.

- Paying bills without running up too much debt.

- Going to work/class every day, or as required, and arriving on time.

- Maintaining a reasonable and healthy food intake.

- Balancing social life and commitments.

- Maintaining a basic level of tidiness and hygiene in their living accommodation.

There are many more complex skills, such as preparing and cooking food, home maintenance, decorating, budgeting and entertaining that they will learn as they go along.

Things that annoy

One of the reasons why parents continue to provide basic services for their young adults is because it is simply easier to do it for them than to have them do it for themselves, especially if they are going to need help or make a mess, and both are possible; however, they need to learn, and parents need to learn to let them. Some degree of chaos tolerance is required as part of the learning process. It may be helpful to begin negotiating a better living arrangement if both parties can compile a list of the things that annoy them about the present circumstances. Ideally, this list should not be used as a way of voicing moans or nagging, but simply a list of things for consideration; for example, one parent's list reads:

- Smells (cooking and personal).

- Mess – at times when it is difficult or inconvenient.

- Cleaning at inopportune moments or in an unusual order, such as before a bath rather than afterwards, washing-up before cooking rather than afterwards.

- Borrowing your things, particularly without asking (car, tights, food, cigarettes, money, makeup, jewellery).

- Lending your things or household things to others.

- Late-night noise.

One young person's list reads:

- Talking all the time, even when I am trying to read.

- Talking to me when I want to be on my own.

- Nagging.

- Telling me off as if I were a five-year-old, particularly in front of my younger siblings or friends.

- Not respecting my privacy; walking into my room without knocking.

- Expecting me to ask permission before I have someone to stay in my room.

- Expecting me to babysit my little brother and sister.

- Expecting me to look after things in the house like helping to decorate the bathroom, but then telling me it's not my house!

- Imposing their way of doing things on me – who says I have to do my laundry twice a week?

Once you have both got your lists, it's time to sit down and be very honest about how you feel, rather than how the other person or people behave, and to negotiate fair and respectful ground rules for living together. Here are a few guiding principles to help you decide what is right and fair for each of you:

- What is reasonable and what is not?

- Is this a privilege or a right?

- Civility and good manners.

- Feeling at home in your own place.

- Public space shared by all.

- The rights to a private space, no matter what state it is in!

TOP TIPS

Help them understand the expectations and responsibilities of living within a family as a young adult:

1 Try not to overwhelm them with services, even if it seems simpler or cheaper to do so. They need to manage their own chores, such as laundry, and even if it means an extra load every week they will never start managing this job for themselves as long as you are willing to do it for them.
2 Keep reminding them that this is a temporary arrangement, even if it does go on for years, and that they will eventually move away to live fully independently and that much as you love them this is also your aim for them.
3 Ensure they feel OK about moving out, but also know that they are welcome to stay – that the choice to go is theirs and theirs alone, and that you will support them to become more independent. Try to find a balance between being clingy and keen to see them go! In cases where young people have become to some degree carers for their parents, those parents need also to be developing their own strategies for independence to enable their young person to make an unhindered choice when they are ready.
4 Bear in mind that you are not duty bound to continue paying for your children for the rest of their lives. It will promote their independence if they realise that they have to earn what they want to spend rather than relying on handouts from you.
5 They need to learn to plan ahead, such as having a clean shirt and underwear for work, enough food to make a meal, posting their own mail and paying their own bills on time, or take the consequences. Don't get involved in their mistakes (but offer support and advice if required).

▶

6 They need to understand that their role with other siblings living at home has changed from being one of the group to one of the adults – and to behave accordingly.

7 All members of a family need to maintain levels of intimacy and affection, and this is done by communication. Whether it's a smile, a hand or pat on the back, or through a chat over a cup of tea once in a while, intimacy and the expression of it needs to be part of every day. This way, smaller issues can be raised and dealt with without problems arising, but it is difficult to chat to someone wearing headphones! Setting time aside for the family to be together, such as Sunday lunch or a family evening, is a good practice to establish and maintain.

HOW YOU FEEL ABOUT BEING TAKEN FOR GRANTED BY YOUR YOUNG PERSON

The big issue here is how much of your personal self is bound up in your role as a parent, and what you consider the role of the parent to be.

The role of the parent usually falls under one of two main functions:

1 **Guidance** Love, care, support, standing up for them, encouraging them.

2 **Management** Shopping, cooking, cleaning, reminding, ensuring they have enough clean clothes to wear.

Unless you are clear about your role with them, and you help them transition into taking on these responsibilities for themselves (so that they can encourage and care for their friends and those they eventually live with), they will not see the end of your management in prospect, and just assume you will continue to do what you have always done.

It's common for emotional relationships between parents and their children to break down during the teenage years. Both parents and children are uncomfortable talking to each other about sensitive issues and tend to talk to their friends instead. It's difficult to chat without passing comment, and such conversations do not sit easily within relationships that are not on an equal footing (you have seen them both helpless and later vulnerable – and they worry you will refer to this in front of others, or just remind them of it). Often the relationship becomes nagging with the parent compensating for this feeling of difficulty by continuing to manage the practical stuff such as cooking and cleaning. Given this background, it's tricky from their point of view for them suddenly to morph into the role of flat sharer. Practice is needed in talking to the young person as an equal and decreasing the amount you do to maintain the status quo at home. It's particularly difficult, because this is being worked out under your roof rather than away from home, and in the process you are changing the environment with which they have grown up.

EXERCISE: Daily tasks and your young person

Think about the following situations and choose your most usual response:

1 Preparing food for them

A They make their own.

B I include them in what I am cooking if I am preparing food for everyone else.

C I will make food just for them, particularly if they have had a hard day and have little time between getting in from work and going out to meet their friends.

2 Cleaning

A They are responsible for cleaning their own space and a share of the communal areas of the property as a whole.

B I vacuum around their room if I am doing the house as a whole, otherwise not.

C I continue to clean their room, as I want the house to be nice.

3 Managing the laundry

A They do their own.

B If I'm loading the machine, and their dirty clothes are in the basket, I will chuck them in too.

C I still manage all the laundry, it's easiest and quickest that way and I am used to the process; it would take too long to explain otherwise.

4 Lifts

A They rely on public transport/their friends for lifts.

B If I am going that way anyway, or a lift for a special occasion is negotiated in advance, I will help.

C I still run them around, as public transport is unreliable and dangerous.

5 Who chooses what is on television?

A We have a majority vote.

B We take turns.

C I let them choose. They tend to leave the room if their choice is not selected, and I would like us all to be together as much as possible.

6 Getting up on time

A It's up to them – they each have an alarm clock.

B I give him one call.

C I wake her up. Jobs are so hard to find, I don't want to risk her getting the sack.

7 Ketchup on the table

A No.

B If appropriate, and part of a tradition, such as with cooked breakfast.

C Eating together is important. Anything that makes it more likely that he will join us is to be encouraged – so I tolerate the ketchup bottle on the table.

So how did you fare?

Mostly As You are living together as independent adults sharing a home, but perhaps there is a point at which you are shutting each other out of your lives. There are plenty of sharers who operate this way, but very few friends who live together do. Perhaps some give and take on both sides would make living together more enjoyable for both of you.

Mostly Bs You seem to have things worked out pretty well, as long as the give and take is not always on your side. Cooperation and collaboration are desirable qualities in a housemate as long as the shared actions are part of your routine anyway. Giving someone a morning call (providing they've asked for one) is an act of kindness, but setting your alarm on a day when you don't have to get up just to wake them is an act of self-sacrifice and going too far.

Mostly Cs You probably feel you are doing your very best for your child, but ironically you are constantly putting your own needs, wants and desires before theirs. You are doing your utmost to stop your child being able to manage without you, and what you think is kindness is actually control and disempowerment. No one wakes up one morning 'finished' and able to function as an adult. Skills and attitudes are learnt and developed. You are hindering your child's development and may be subtly sabotaging their future relationships too.

How far do you 'let go' as you provide accommodation for your children?

A really difficult issue for the avoidance of Hotel Mum and Dad is how far you are willing to 'let go'. It's an important, but difficult, realisation that life does not have to be done your way, just because it has been done that way up until now. Letting them make changes, and doing things in a different way, can be revitalising when you accept them – and if you think back, you will find examples of when you had to do something similar.

EXERCISE: Being prepared to make changes yourself

Do you remember how it felt when you had to:

• Accommodate how Christmas is managed when a new partnership is formed.

• Accept that there are things you like to eat or watch that your partner does not?

- Learn to tolerate a range of different assumptions, from political affiliations to allegiances to a particular supermarket within a family you join that are different from those you have grown up with?

Perhaps this will remind you of how strange it felt. Making changes means letting go of a huge part of who you are, but you can find yourself taking pleasure in new things and creating new interests and a new identity for yourself. But the experiences of our young people, perhaps when studying or travelling, can expand our universe, and help us realise how limited our horizons have been.

QUESTIONS AND ANSWERS

Q: 'My daughter is about to come home to live after the break-up of her relationship. The trouble is that in the process she is downsizing from a flat to a room and a share of our house, and she wants to bring furniture with her. In the meantime, we have downsized from the family house to a flat, and although we have a spare bedroom that she can use, there simply isn't room for all her stuff.'

A: Suggest that part of the ending of her relationship offers the chance to think about slimming down the possessions that went with it. You cannot be expected to have room for all her belongings whenever she decides to return to you for an unending period. Suggest she really thinks about what she wants to keep, how much space there is in the accommodation you have to offer, and gives what she does not want to retain to a charity, or pays for storage in one of the relatively low-cost storage facilities that are springing up all over (that will really make her think about what she wants to keep). If you do have room, say in the loft or a garage, it should be her and her friends who help her manage the shifting and lifting. Storing your children's stuff should not also become an impediment to moving on with your life – perhaps downsizing further, choosing to change your living arrangements to involve an elderly relative, or moving away.

Q: 'My son lives at home and will regularly bring friends home for dinner and expect me to feed them. It's partly my own fault, because when they were little I always said I didn't mind who came home for tea. He's grown up with me accepting his friends, but now I feel rather taken for granted – and in any case cooking a few extra fish fingers is rather different from suddenly feeding three additional adults.'

A: You probably like the fact that your son feels comfortable about asking people home, but if it has turned into a chore and an expectation, to be served up without prior warning, then it has perhaps gone too far. Encourage continued attendance if you like, but ask for warning, and a contribution – he could make part of the meal he is keen that they share, for example. Also, as they are keen on joining a meal in a family home, make it just that – and make it a family meal, to which they contribute with attention and good conversation (with mobile phones switched off!).

CHAPTER 10

Expecting the Unexpected

Finding out that your child has either unexpectedly become pregnant or fathered a potential child can be a shock for all involved. Our starting point is that this should be an important life journey that you support them through, rather than one you manage and try to minimise on their behalf. Of course, it can be disappointing to see your young person having to grow up more quickly than anyone expected and to have to make choices not previously considered. If the situation is taken out of their hands, however, so is the associated responsibility, and they may end up learning nothing from a very serious situation but feeling a great deal of unresolved emotion.

As research into family history grows, and more people investigate family secrets, it has become relatively common for adults to find out that their much older sister was in fact their mother, or the departure of an older sibling who was putting on weight was in fact preparation for birth and adoption. Although the secrecy and deception are no longer common, it remains tempting to absorb an unexpected child within the wider family, so that the life planned out for a young person can proceed with as little interruption as possible.

One of the consequences of the change in attitudes within society towards single parents and blended families is a marked difference in the approach taken by parents, depending on whether their unplanned expectant parent is male or female. In previous generations young men were expected to 'do the right thing' (not that everyone did). These days, young women neither expect nor want an unwilling partner, but most would still very much like to have a willing one.

Regrettably, it's still often the young woman who is quite literally 'left holding the baby' and the young man meanwhile being encouraged to 'get on with his plans' rather than tie himself down with the financial, emotional and physical commitment of being a parent, regardless of whether or not he also chooses to be a partner. The fact that it is the mother who bears the child usually means that the decision to proceed with or terminate the pregnancy is considered to be hers, but this may also leave the father feeling powerless and excluded from the decision-making process – particularly if they are no longer together. If the decision reached is not to his liking, he may feel even more marginalised and hurt.

Although it might be sad and painful to see your young person suddenly faced with difficult choices, you need to help them work their way through the situation. With choices come responsibilities, and the choice to be involved in a sexual relationship is never without risk.

EARLY DAYS

In Britain today the average age of first sexual intercourse is 16, which means that approximately half of all young people will have sex before or during their sixteenth year, and many are quite a bit older. Although many parents are aware of their child's sexual development and take care to talk with them frankly about contraception, others, through denial or embarrassment, prefer to believe that their child is too young and falls into the 'later' category. Of course, even if you have prepared your child well and frequently discuss sexual health issues, contraception is never 100 per cent reliable, and heterosexual sex always carries with it the possibility of pregnancy. Although use of emergency contraception – often known as the 'morning-after pill' – is an effective way to help ensure that an unprotected sexual act or a condom failure don't result in a continuing pregnancy, many parents are either lacking in knowledge or simply don't talk enough to their young person about the availability and advisability of its use.

Should you ever find yourself in a situation where your young person admits to having unprotected sex, remember that the morning-after pill can be used for up to 72 hours, although it is more effective the sooner it is used. Emergency contraception can be obtained from GPs, pharmacies (including those in supermarkets) and health clinics free of charge to young people.

Being a young person often means a way of looking at the world through a lens of optimism and believing that the unthinkable cannot happen to them – which may make it all the harder to accept when that unthinkable consequence occurs. If accepting the reality and consequences of a pregnancy is unavoidable – as it is for the pregnant young woman – there may be stages of anger, denial, blame, regret and even depression that follow once the pregnancy is confirmed, and these may mean that the young woman keeps her pregnancy secret for some time. In some families, a daughter will confide in her parents almost at once with the hope that somehow they will be able to make it all right for her, but whether she experiences the 'it's not happening' or the 'mummy make it go away' reaction, a parent's job is to help her move into the mature acceptance stage, because it is only here that she will be able to make life decisions that she will not later regret.

For a young man, the reaction may be similar but, unlike his partner, he may be in a position where he can simply walk away, particularly if he has no strong relationship with her. He may even deny the baby is his, or accuse her of entrapment, both of which may add to her mental distress and result in a decision by the young woman to exclude him from further involvement in order to preserve her own well-being.

As a parent, being told by your young person that a pregnancy has been confirmed can be devastating when so many hours of loving care have gone into preparing them for a very different future. Your first reaction may be anger or blame, but given that the time for contraception has long gone, un-wishing the sex that produced the newly growing life is not helpful. Two people are jointly responsible for its creation, it's a life-changing event for them both, and they will both now need love, support and encouragement to help them chart their way through the difficult decisions ahead.

When confronted with this new reality, the best thing any parent can do is simply listen, offer loving support and reassurance that no matter what decisions are made, your love and support for them will never be withdrawn – even though it may take you a while to readjust your view of their future. Over the next few days, a lot of honest talk needs to happen between the young woman and young man – as well as with their parents – but this should not be forced. Give them time and space, because they too are probably very confused at the moment.

Considerations before any decisions are made

It's a good idea to support your young person by drawing up a list of questions, suggestions, options and information that will help to make the choices clearer. Here are some of the things you might consider:

- Contacting your daughter's head of year, if she is still at school, to have a confidential conversation about the school's position in relation to continuing studies while pregnant.

- Checking out the local council for information and support for pregnant young women. There should be advice available as well as groups, childcare advice and guidance on benefits. Look on your council website or talk to the local Citizens Advice Bureau.

  If your daughter is at university or college, encourage her to find out the possibility of deferment, so that she can take time out of her studies and rejoin the course a year later as well as seeing if there is a crèche facility or nursery available.

- Making an appointment with a reliable pregnancy-advisory agency, but be careful because many agencies that advertise themselves as young people's advice agencies come with an agenda or are funded by a religious organisation, which might lead to considerable bias; for example, there are instances of pregnant young women being shown photographs of dead foetuses. Ideally, both the potential mother and father should attend together, but if this is not possible then encourage your daughter to take a friend with them rather than you.

- Looking at the local childcare options and prices.

Throughout this process, and the discussions you will be having together while completing your investigations, resist any temptation to give your opinion on what should happen next, even if asked. It can be very difficult to see a child having to change their plans for a glowing future if you are in favour of a termination, and likewise it can be devastating if you are eagerly anticipating a grandchild when your child tells you they want an abortion. No matter what your personal feelings, they are the ones who have to live with this decision for the rest of their lives, and they have to make it for themselves.

By the end of this process it will be possible to have some idea of the associated costs, the price of the different options and, therefore, how much of a financial contribution will be expected from each young person. For a young man, this can come as a shock, particularly if he envisaged life going on as normal except for occasional baby visits. A young man may well find that he now needs to change his plans too in order to provide money, so he may need to think about part-time work or changing education from full-time to part-time and generally cutting down his costs.

Choosing not to be a parent – abortion and adoption

This section is not intended to offer moral advice on abortion or adoption, rather to explain the options and raise the likely logistical and emotional consequences.

Abortion

Depending on when the young woman finds out about her pregnancy, there are various options for abortion.

1 Abortion to end a pregnancy becomes a more complicated and invasive process as the pregnancy progresses. Advice can be obtained from your GP or health centres such as Brook or the British Pregnancy Advisory Service (BPAS).

2 There are two main ways in which an abortion takes place; either by a surgical intervention through which the foetus is removed by a vacuum from the uterus (under either local or general anaesthetic) or by the use of medication known as the abortion pill.

3 The abortion pill consists of two medicines taken between six hours and three days apart, which induce a miscarriage. The British Pregnancy Advisory Service (www.bpas.org) will administer the abortion pill up to 23 weeks and 5 days into a pregnancy,

although the later it is administered the more painful and trau-
matic the resultant miscarriage might be.

4   For a pregnancy up to nine weeks, the miscarriage takes place
    at home and is similar to an ordinary menstrual period for most
    women. If later than nine weeks, a nurse would be in atten-
    dance until the process is complete, at which point the young
    person is free to go home.

5   Surgical abortion is usually carried out as a day patient, so no
    overnight stay is required and can be either with a local anaes-
    thetic (up to 12 weeks) or a general anaesthetic (up to 15 weeks).
    For pregnancies over 15 weeks, a slightly more involved process
    is required although usually not requiring an overnight stay.
    Over 20 weeks and the time in hospital may be longer.[18]

Whatever your feelings about the pregnancy, and the consequences you anticipate, it is not a good idea for you to put
pressure on the young people making this decision. What has
happened has already interrupted the life they had planned, and
having the decision about what to do next taken out of their
hands – even if they ask for it – may result in confusion now and
resentment later in life.

Counselling may be helpful, in a non-judgemental way, for all
involved – the two principals and even both sets of parents,
although probably not together. But the outcome does need to
feel like the decision of those principally involved. Lifelong guilt
and resentment can result if they feel this was not the right
choice, or if they feel they were forced into a decision too soon or
against their will. If the atmosphere within the family is too
heated for open debate, talking to a sexual-health counsellor or
adviser is essential, but bear in mind that counselling available
from other agencies may often come with a particular agenda,
based on moral or religious principles, and even entering the por-
tals of an associated organisation may result in the young person
having to become aware of how strongly complete strangers feel

about the dilemma they are facing. Whatever they decide, they may emerge scarred by the experience.

As the grandparent of the life being considered, you will undoubtedly have strong feelings, but you need to think about how to resource your needs separately from those of your young person. It's not a good idea to make them responsible for your feelings too. Talk to your friends if you know they won't share details of your child's situation with others, or talk to a counsellor yourself, with your partner if you have one. Lost grandchildren can be hard to talk about but can cause a profound shift in the relationships within a family and strain the familial intimacy as time passes.

If an abortion is chosen, as parents you may be tempted to try to encourage your young person to move on with their life and 'forget it ever happened'. However kindly this is meant, it is probably impossible to achieve – and may not necessarily be desirable in any case. The young people involved will have feelings about what happened, and the choices they made, which may include sadness, guilt or depression mixed with relief and even euphoria that life is back to normal for them. They may try to act as if nothing happened in order to manage their feelings, but this is not generally held to be a healthy way to deal with an emotional event like this. In the months and years to come you could perhaps gently, and without blaming, promote the occasional conversation about what occurred, and the feelings they have now, looking back, as well as sharing some of your own – including of course your love and pride in them for getting on with their lives.

Adoption

Adoption is another way of managing an unplanned pregnancy, although one that is taken much less regularly today. Adoption is worth considering when there is an ethical problem with abortion but a clear desire not to become a parent at this time in their lives.

Now that abortion is readily available and the social stigma of single-parenthood is so much reduced, there are many fewer adoptions than in previous times. Evidence suggests that it is best for a child to be adopted from birth, but relatively few take place at this time – most are before the age of four. Legal procedures mean that even when a baby is placed from birth with its prospective new adoptive parents, the birth parents can have their child returned up until the final court proceedings, which take approximately three to four months from placement. Parents who are unsure can opt to have their child fostered from birth until they are ready to make a decision, although this might not always be in the child's best interests.

If considering adoption, it would be a good idea to talk to a professional – a social worker, health professional or someone working for an adoption agency – about what happens and when, and as early as possible, as the less psychological bonding that takes place, the easier the process of transfer may prove to be. If the father is named on the birth certificate, he must also give his permission for an adoption. Although he cannot insist that the mother takes custody of the child, he may choose to bring the child up himself. If no father is mentioned on the birth certificate, then the mother's decision is all that is required.

The British Association for Adoption and Fostering has an excellent website with lots of information on the adoption and fostering processes at www.baaf.org.uk

PRACTICAL ISSUES TO DO WITH PREGNANCY

If the pregnancy is to continue, there will be practical issues to address. Depending on the age of the parents, there will questions about the extent to which education should be interrupted, the level of provision made by local authorities for crèches and other support, and physical issues like where the new arrival is to sleep and be cared for.

State schools in the UK generally do what they can to help pregnant students stay in education and complete their exams. In general, they will not permanently exclude a young woman just because she is pregnant and will often seek to offer both support and educational consistency. Pregnant girls will usually be allowed to attend school for their classes and associated examinations, although as the anticipated delivery date approaches they may prefer to study from home rather than attend school or college.

It may be preferable to take a year out of formal education altogether. Although this might sound tempting, dropping down to be with another year group can be a big issue for the young person, and if it is possible to keep going and avoid breaking the education, then statistics show there is less risk of completely giving up. If they do have to temporarily drop out of school, encourage them to keep in touch with their studies, their classmates and perhaps keep up to date with wider reading around their subjects so that they retain their former ambitions. Tutors will generally be sympathetic to this and will usually provide reading lists or coursework if asked.

If a departure for university was scheduled, and a pregnancy has now interrupted the plan, then perhaps a place at a university closer to home might be an attractive solution; a daily commute planned to a different institution or the option deferred for a year. Universities will take into account all your circumstances when allocating and offering accommodation, and many have units that will suit (single) parents with accompanying services such as crèches and childcare support.

Do think carefully before agreeing that a young person can leave their child at home with its grandparents while they go off to study. In the long run this can lead to heartache for the grandparents, who have had responsibilities but not rights, and disassociation for the child, who is not quite sure who is their parent. If, after considering their options, your young person chooses to become a parent, then this is what they need to become. The parents' role is to help them but not to take the burden off their shoulders by assuming it yourselves.

If the pregnancy is to be managed from the young person's family home, you will need to think about accommodation, and who will sleep where. Putting up a partition can create an instant and separate space within even a small room and help the young person prepare for the birth. It is important to know from the outset that a young person living with their baby with a parent or parents will not get preferential housing treatment in most areas unless they are homeless or threatened with homelessness. Even then, they may well only be offered bed-and-breakfast accommodation or hostel accommodation.

The launch of the Access card in the UK proposed that the credit card helped a mother 'do the best for her baby', enabling her to buy large amounts of equipment, but in reality much of the apparatus can be managed without, secured second hand or received free from those who no longer need it. There are plenty of sites offering free samples for babies, usually when you register with them, or discounts and offers galore. EBay, Gumtree and other sites have a huge amount of very cheap items for sale, many almost new, from babies who have outgrown clothes, prams and sets long before the items are worn out.

There are benefits to which a young parent is entitled and they may need your help in understanding their legal and financial position. It is not always easy to find what their entitlements might be, so encourage them to talk to their social worker or health adviser, look at websites or visit your Citizens Advice Bureau. The amount of benefit that any young person will get depends on their circumstances, and fathers are expected to support their child financially – even if they are not financially independent.

Because of these financial expectations, many young men will dispute their paternity, and a quick glance at websites designed for young fathers will show that some of them operate on the premise that without proof you don't have to pay a penny! Of course, if a young man wants proof of paternity he is entitled to it, although depending on the relationship between a couple it might prove emotionally difficult for a young pregnant woman who is already dealing with the challenges of family and friendship changes, educational issues, hormones and finances to be asked to provide a sample for testing from the person she considers to be her partner.

DNA testing can be carried out to prove paternity through various channels, including home testing kits (although these should not be considered suitable for building a legal case to deny involvement and responsibility for the child they have helped to create). Involving lawyers in what could be more reasonably discussed can over-complicate the issue and result in excessive costs. A blank on a birth certificate can leave long-term consequences for all involved.

EARLY PARENTHOOD FROM YOUR POINT OF VIEW

We have acknowledged this can be a shock, and finding your son or daughter faced with sudden, life-changing decisions can be profoundly distressing. But the changes to your life also need to be acknowledged – even if you feel selfish or guilty thinking of them right now. You may have been looking forward to a greater level of independence now that your children are grown up – travelling, maybe downsizing your accommodation – and achieving greater financial security. Finding these plans put on hold can be destabilising.

Fathers, in particular, may struggle with the joint realisations that not only is their little girl sexually active but she is also about to make him a grandfather, resulting in a change of life that feels over-abrupt and instantly ageing. A threatened return to sleepless nights, nappies and the endless cycle of washing can produce a feeling of being trapped, newly encircled by the demands of a small child when you have already been through that stage in your life. Just as you were heading for a simpler, easier life – with fewer responsibilities and more chance to enjoy things – you find yourself required to deliver both practical and material support all over again. In such circumstances, resentments can brew, especially if Grandma-to-be is suddenly entering into the nesting phase with gusto, leaving her partner isolated and unable to express his feelings across the hormone divide. It is not at all unusual in such circumstances to find him spending more and more time away from the family home indulging in hobbies and the company of men in general – and if he is particularly insecure, possibly other women too.

The mother of an expectant young person too may experience a loss of identity, mourning for the future you had planned, for both yourself and your young person. Some, on the other hand, may greet the new arrival as a welcome return to the most significant role of your life – as a mother. Instead of going through the process of redefining yourself and your life, this new circumstance might act as a delayer of thought and action, a reason for deferring wider consideration of what to do with your future as you thoroughly involve yourself in the next generation. Accepting responsibility for the next generation, whether or not you would have chosen this route, can be an entirely practical response to the mourning that can come with a realisation that your nest really is empty.

Many women with a young parent and their child at home will 'just help them to live their lives as a normal young person' by doing far more childcare and babysitting than an average grandparent. After all, the child is living in the same home, so it is hardly babysitting when mum is staying in, if a young parent is off out with their friends. You would probably not expect your child to pay for a babysitter when you are sitting downstairs watching television, but if you are sharing your home with your child and a baby, you may need to make more effort than usual to have an independent life away from home. Your young person also needs the space to explore what it means to be a parent and the time to make a proper bond with their child.

No matter how hard it is to see your child giving up her youth to care for her baby, she needs to be making her own arrangements and decisions, not trying to live the life of a 'foot-loose and fancy free' young person who just happens to have a baby at home. Learning to be responsible can only happen if one takes on responsibility, so for a parent of a young person, saying no or expecting them to make suitable arrangements is in the long run doing them a favour.

For the parent of a young man with a child, the desire to see your grandchild can outweigh your desire to remain neutral within their relationship to each other. Many paternal grandparents will offer to take a child for a night, a weekend or even longer, simply because they don't get the opportunity to see their grandchild at any other time or in any other circumstance. This can be really hard as you may find yourself being used, and even blackmailed, if you want to maintain any kind of relationship. Being willing to provide care, but being very clear about the boundaries, is probably best for everyone – as will be having a strong sense of your own identity and developing your independent life away from the family. All will help your child show more respect and provide you with a more meaningful future.

Of course, even more difficult might be the plight of grandparents who have no access to their grandchild, where the broken relationship of their own child blocks access to the baby. The absence of photographs, information, access to important milestones in your grandchild's life can be literally heart-breaking – for both you and your wider family, as your young person's siblings are also denied involvement in their niece or nephew. You do, however, have some choices. You cannot insist that the mother of the child includes you in their life, but you can offer care and support, even if your child wants nothing to do with the baby. Be aware, however, that any contact can be withdrawn at a moment's notice without any recourse to law on your side. The situation can work, and there are many children growing up with grandparents, aunts and uncles from their biological father's side – even if they do not know their father.

In summary, this is a complicated area that plays havoc with so many previously unchallenged boundaries and expectations, hopes and dreams and requires some very difficult decisions. But, as you guide your young person to accept the situation, make appropriate plans and live with the consequences, you will be helping them grow up.

QUESTIONS AND ANSWERS

Q: 'My daughter had a baby at 17 and is now 20, living on her own with the child, and very prone to depression. There are signs her condition is worsening and I am very worried about them both. Should I invite them home to live with me?'
A: A short-term, emergency stay with you might be a good solution for a while, as long as it is supported by the stated expectation that she resumes her independence and returns to her life in the longer term. Managing expectations can help both parties plan ahead, and so if you could tie your offer of accommodation to a particular season, it might help both of you – 'you might like to come and stay with us until after Christmas/the New Year/the end of the school holidays'.

Support her in taking care of her child, but try not to take over – becoming the mother to two girls may not help her in the longer term. Instead, helping her to maintain a sense of herself as a responsible adult may assist her in reasserting her independence.

Q: 'Having left for university only last October, our daughter is now pregnant and will shortly be returning home at the end of her first year, just before the baby is due. Her intention is to take a year out of her university course and return again in due course, with her child. I grieve for how she must feel – returning home so soon after she left – and the problem is made worse because our house is small and space is at a premium. How can we give her some sense of independence when we know this is not an ideal situation and not what she really wants to do?'

A: Assuming the decision to return home has been mutually agreed, and seems best for all, in reality space can be carved out of the smallest houses – a curtain rail across a ceiling can divide a room in two, and plasterboard partitions are relatively simple to establish. If you have a garage, this could be turned into an additional room for a relatively low cost.

Within the kitchen, allocating her a cupboard for food, and not insisting that she eat at the same time as everyone else can preserve a sense of her independence, as can altering the routine for when she arrives home. Allowing her to enter the house and her own space, and no longer expecting her to talk about her day the moment she arrives, may help her to realise that you don't assume things have returned to the normality she so recently left.

In the longer term, she sounds focused and mature – and supporting her determination to return to university will be appreciated.

Q: 'My husband says that if our daughter has the baby she is expecting, she is not to come home, that it's a question of him or her. What should I do?'

A: It sounds as if he is frightened of the challenge facing you, and about what will happen, but drawing up lines of battle, and requiring allegiances to be stated is not going to help. Can you – or someone else close to you – draw your husband out about how he feels and why he is making such a dramatic proposal? No one should be required to make a choice between their partner and their child, and decisions based on this situation are unlikely to be viewed as reasonable in future.

Another option is to try expressing your situation through the lives of others – perhaps superimposing it on friends who have children of a similar age. Soap operas and plots of novels dealing with similar issues can be very helpful. Explain the situation slowly, from someone else's position, and see how he feels then.

Of course, he is distressed, as the life he was planning free from children has just disappeared, but now more than ever he needs to know how much you all love and need his help and support.

Above all, encourage him to take time to consider and not to make decisions that will have life-long consequences if made in a hurry. Requiring his child to make such a choice in order to comply with a higher diktat could be a source of great resentment in future – and lead to him losing the love and respect not only of his daughter but also his grandchild.

Q: 'My son has just told us the girl he was seeing is pregnant. He was due to go to university in two months and I think it's a terrible shame for him to give up his dreams for a girl he hardly knows.'
A: How well he knows her is not the issue. He knew her well enough to be 50 per cent responsible for the conception, and he needs to acknowledge his responsibility. Rather than encouraging him to walk away, which could hardly be behaviour you would admire in an adult, try to talk to him about the consequences – and how to live up to the responsibilities he has already assumed. This is obviously not a situation you are going to be overjoyed about, but shutting the door on this young woman and her child is not the answer. Having a son who is following his dreams would make any mother proud, but having a son who lives up to his responsibilities and is a good father to his own child should make her even prouder!

If he really doubts that the baby is his, he has the right to have a paternity test.

CHAPTER 11

To Infinity and Beyond

This final chapter looks at how you move from being a parent of a young person towards being more of a friend, and how you form a friendly relationship between two connected adults that can be a source of pleasure and support to you both in the future.

This may feel an odd way to end our book. After all, we've been fond of saying that parents should aim to parent their young people rather than befriend them, but there will come a time when the young people are mature, and separate, enough for the relationship to move on, and for you to establish a new way of communicating. Although the link you share will always be grounded in their initial dependency, and your shared history, the relationship you establish at this stage can henceforth proceed as one between consenting – and mutually contributing – adults, and hopefully a source of profound satisfaction to both of you.

CHANGE FROM THE YOUNG
PERSON'S POINT OF VIEW

What do young adults want from their parents?

Advice when they want it, not when the parent wants to give it. Young adults are likely to want you to be an occasional resource for support and advice rather than a constant commentary on everything they do. If you are aware that they are approaching a big decision, perhaps you could ask them questions to help guide their thinking rather than come up with a ready-made decision that all they have to do is implement. The best advice may be to bite your tongue until you are asked.

Ongoing encouragement and applause. In a world that is short of encouragement, and where doing well can attract negative vibes, even from so-called friends, most of us want affirmation from our parents – and on a life-long basis. This may include keeping relatives up to date with their news in an appropriate manner (such as not sharing all the difficult details about the insecurities of the journey, but rather announcing the broad headlines of the outcome). They want you to support their development. They also want you to be proud of them.

You to fit in with them rather than them having to fit around you and to be pleased to see them when they decide to be in touch rather than showering them with helpful hints on what they could have done 'had they been more thoughtful'.

What *don't* young adults want from their parents?

To be reminded of mistakes they made as a child or teenager and have these mapped onto their current lives, as if they were pre-destined to make them all over again, repeatedly.

For you to remember every specific detail of what they have told you in the past, and to be asked about these things again, when they are trying to forget or move on.

To have their sense of discovery diminished. Even if the things they tell you are commonplace, or you went through – and, frankly, more effectively managed – similar things at the same age, hold back on sharing your greater wisdom. Be surprised, delighted and impressed. Allow them to tell you something!

To be over-involved in the dramas of your life, with you giving them more detail than they really want or need.

For you to crowd them out with so much eventful information on what you are doing that their own life feels poorly furnished by comparison.

To be nagged.

To feel guilty for not thinking about you, seeing you or including you in what they are doing.

Although these are natural stages and common feelings, separating from parents is part of the process of growing up, and it can have the almost inevitable consequence of parent(s) feeling temporarily marginalised. But rather than feeling sad, it's helpful for you to take pride in having raised an independent young person who is managing life on their own. This gets easier with practice.

Why can't they just be more in touch? After all, you are not that old!

You may wonder why a 20-something person cannot be more friendly and considerate to someone in their fifties, but the reality is that not many 20-year-olds have friends who are in their fifties. Given time, this may change, particularly once they start working and are brought into contact with people of all ages as colleagues and equals. Your lives may converge again, perhaps when they settle down, establish a relationship or have children of their own. Although many of the things they will experience you have already been through – and you could save them time and trouble by telling them what you found out on the way – your learning won't do for both them and you, they have to experience it themselves. Parents remember being the age they are now, whereas their children are going through it for the first time.

Promoting good communication

Don't expect – rather, be loving and supportive. Acknowledge the positive rather than harping on about the negative, how much you enjoyed their visit rather than how much longer you wished it could have lasted.

Don't anticipate set piece scenes – 'I had just imagined us all doing this'. Rather, take pleasure in moments that occur. Be in the moment. Last suppers before departures or recreating key moments in family life can be particularly stressful – remember to note what does take place and to enjoy it rather than regret that it's not what you had envisaged.

Don't provide comparisons. The neighbour's immense good fortune in receiving a surprise cruise to celebrate her significant birthday may not be the most tactful story to tell.

Develop shared activities that involve both parties and can be enjoyed together – researching family history, clearing out their room with them or encouraging them to store in the loft things that they might want to have in future, getting them to help you with a specific job such as redecorating.

Keep an eye on the family safety valves, the little things that make them feel safe and secure, such as a particular walk or take-away when they are home. Say that you'd love their company rather than that they are obliged to do this.

Being willing to adapt certain traditions – such as Christmas or Thanksgiving – and include new people in new ways. Being inclusive, rather than exclusive, and willing to adapt is a great way of encouraging them to share their new life.

Sending communication for the pleasure of keeping in touch, rather than coating it with a grudging expectation that it will be responded to within a similar time frame. If they feel that communication is loaded with expectation and it makes them feel guilty, they are less likely to get in touch or to be honestly themselves when they do.

Make conversations easy, so that when you ring each other it's for the pure pleasure of talking rather than that either of you has an agenda to talk through. Get into the habit of exchanging news and being glad to hear what they have been doing rather than turning each activity you hear into a reason why they have not been to see you.

Be discreet Passing on rumours of what you heard they said to other relatives, and your strong reactions, may well get back to them and will promote long-term disharmony. They will be much less open with you in future.

Taking this further, if you would like to make the relationship more like it would be between friends, then behave like friends. From workshops with all ages the top ten qualities and skills of a good friend include:

- **Confidentiality** Keeping sensitive information private, including changes in relationships, hopes and aspirations, problems, upsets and embarrassments.

- **Discretion** Answering questions from others without revealing or inferring issues of confidence.

- **Loyalty** Being on your side, no matter what (even when you have behaved poorly, as no one needs another conscience).

- **Listening** Being willing to listen without turning the conversation on to the self, but not getting stuck in deep emotion all the time.

- **Supporting** Lending a hand when needed, giving a reality check when needed, giving hugs and affectionate contact the rest of the time.

- **Forgiving** When everything has been said and done.

- **Letting go of the past** As old transgressions or unkindnesses are forgotten.

- **Having a sense of humour** This is probably very high on most young people's list of desirable qualities, particularly being able to laugh at yourself.

- **Showing patience** Some people need to repeat mistakes quite a few times before they move on.

- **Being reliable** and always there when you need them.

Relaxing your expectations about how much you know about your young person's life

One of the other areas over which parents often express a feeling of loss – and a desire to reinstate – is the level of intimacy they experience with their young person. When a child is young, a parent is often the key confidant, and even during the turbulence of adolescence many parents still remain someone their child can, if they choose, talk to about almost anything.

As they grow older and develop lives separate from their family, and perhaps find a partner or a strong friendship circle, their need for their parent(s) will often change. In some families parents are still kept in mind and loved and cherished, but the young people may increasingly withhold much of their emotional life, their intimate self, from the relationship. They may continue to report back on what they have done and where they have been, but not necessarily the inner glories and struggles of their lives, which they may share with others. The reasons for this may be various: would you listen? Would you pass judgement? Would you never forget it, wishing they had not told you?

When young people and adults on Gill's workshops have been asked to identify the qualities or actions of a listener that make it possible to discuss sensitive issues, there are key responses that emerge. A good listener is someone who:

- Has time to talk.

- Has appropriate facial expressions, open body language, is genuinely interested and shows it, is prepared to listen and not just suggest solutions, is trustworthy – holds appropriate confidentiality and shows care.

- Gives good advice.

- Is not judgemental.

- Is honest.

- Is calm.

- Is understanding.

- Is responsive and reassuring, reasonable and offers suggestions and choices.

- Can focus on the speaker and doesn't keep bringing the issue back to themselves.

- Will let go of the topic once it's over and not keep asking in the future.

CHANGE FROM THE PARENT'S
POINT OF VIEW

The challenge for parents at this time is to think about how you pick up your life and make it satisfying for you rather than dependent on your role as a parent.

It's important to invest in positive thinking. Rather than feeling sadness that your role as a parent seems to have ended now that you are no longer needed on a daily basis, you could concentrate on having the time and energy to do new things, to pick up activities and friends that were previously unmanageable within the constraints of raising a family. Take pride in the fact that you have created an independent and successful young person rather than dwelling on sadness that they are not the person they once were. Concentrate on what they do rather than what they do not do, and delete from your vocabulary, 'The least they could do is . . .' Parenting does not create a debt; the decision to have them was yours and they really don't owe you. Everything you did for them was a choice you made for you.

Look at your own life and your own friendships and work towards creating a pattern that stimulates and interests you so that you have interesting things to tell them too.

Don't expect them to feel responsible for you, or try to make them so. There will almost certainly be a time in the relationship when they will have to take some responsibility for you – perhaps due to a future severe illness or at the end of your life, and they will probably have to arrange your funeral and sort out your estate – but this will work best if they have been acknowledged as an independent person first. If this transition is not managed well, there may be unresolved issues later on. They are not responsible for your happiness in the home they have left behind, they don't have to 'make it up to you' that they have left, and if you imply this they will feel burdened.

A very important stage in demonstrating that you accept that they are grown up and independent is allowing them to show that they know more about things than you do. They almost certainly do – particularly about technology – but if you acknowledge them as a source of information and value what they have to tell you, this can be a very important way of growing the relationship.

Overall, this is an odd stage in life. Realising that the next generation is now making their way without us, and that the torch has been passed to them, can certainly make us all feel stale, old and out of date. But in the long run, managing this stage well can yield a really valuable asset to take forward – a worthwhile relationship that can be a source of pleasure and nourishment for years to come. There is nothing worth more care and attention. Bear in mind that most of us in death are defined not by what we achieved but by who loved us ('son of x, partner of y, father of z').

One final irony: for many of us, no sooner have our children left than our parents start to need help and support. It can be a potential source of frustration when anticipating an unencumbered future. But remember that if our children don't owe us a debt, neither are we indebted to our parents. What is given should be done freely and lovingly out of our concern and care, not from guilt or duty. Of course, this does not mean we will always be thrilled to visit or spend an hour discussing symptoms or treatments on the phone, and perhaps we are entitled to feel a little put out once in a while. It's worth remembering that how we respond to our parents as they become less independent is likely to model how our children will respond to us when the time comes.

CASE STUDY: ISOBEL, 46

Isobel has two children: Jonathan, 24, and Emma, 22. Isobel has been raising her children alone since Jonathan was about ten, after the relationship with their father broke down, and she has been single ever since. Jonathan is now working and living in South Africa and intends to stay for the foreseeable future, and Isobel was devastated when Emma, after briefly returning from university, landed a job working for a big hotel in China.

After a period of feeling lost and alone, she started to look at all the things she had wanted to do but was unable to because of her family commitments. With the help of friends, she created a three-year life plan, which included starting a part-time degree course, changing her job and revitalising her social life by joining a range of different clubs and societies, such as a book club, a film club and a local-history society, all of which she found online.

She is in regular contact with her son via Facebook and email, and she Skypes with her daughter at least once a week, where they have lots to talk about. She is hoping to be able to visit both children, with some assistance from them, in the next 18 months or so. Although she misses them very much, she has whole new elements to her life that are exciting and stimulating

QUESTIONS AND ANSWERS

Q: 'I want my daughter to clear out her room. She has now finished university, embarked on her first job, and has her own flat – but she still keeps her room as it was in our home, and it's full of all her stuff. I feel I can't move on with my life until she does.'
A: This needs discussion. She has embarked on her next stage but is effectively asking you to hold her old life as a museum piece within her family home, and you might have other plans –

including living somewhere else. Although it's you that wants the stuff moved, it's important that she takes responsibility for it – and if you do it for her you risk accusations later on. If there is room for storage at home, maybe you could help her pack up what she wants to keep and store it in the attic, or get rid of what she no longer needs by helping her take it to charity shops. Alternatively, if there is stuff she really wants to keep, but no one has room for, she could consider taking space in one of the storage units that are now available.

Q: 'Our 24-year-old son never phones or comes to visit us. He says he is too busy. On the rare occasions that I do see him, he never tells me anything – and I don't even know whether or not he has a girlfriend.'

A: Although on the face of it you may feel hurt that he shares so little of himself and his life, a good starting place would be to think about why he doesn't tell you more. Does he find your questions invasive? Does he worry that if he answers you, once you have information you will constantly refer back to it and leave him wishing you did not know? Or does he worry that if he tells you a little that you will start prying further, or try to advise him?

A good way to deal with this might be to show him that it's possible for the two of you to have contact without it being heavy. Suggest a trip to the theatre or to see a film, do something together rather than requiring him to talk. Involve other people – and if he opens up with a wider audience, don't resentfully point out later how chatty he was with them, rather than his usual monosyllabic conversation. Send him the occasional email or postcard to keep him up to date with your news. And try to congratulate yourself on raising an independent young person who may reconnect with you later on – once he has gone through the process of demonstrating that he is independent.

Q: 'My elderly father is always complaining that he doesn't see enough of his grandchildren. The problem is that he relies on me

to mediate the relationship rather than managing it himself. Being required to remind my children to contact him is an ongoing burden and I end up resenting being in the middle and feeling guilty that they don't remember to communicate with him more.'
A: The relationship between grandparents and grandchildren can be precious, but if it is to be meaningful it needs to be contributed to by both sides, not just by relying on someone in the middle. Does your father ever contact his grandchildren directly? If not, encourage him to be in touch with them himself. Provide him with a list of their mobile numbers and most recent postal addresses. If he is online, then suggest they exchange email addresses. Along the same lines, you might consider giving your children a list of family birthdays so that they can send a card on the right day – often hugely appreciated – or despatch a postcard when they are away.

Many older people want to be seen as the patriarch or matriarch of the family, and to be accorded associated deference and respect, communicated with at regular intervals, consulted for their opinion, and not required to do any of the relationship management themselves. Although this approach might have worked when they were the grandchildren, society today is much less reverential of age, and their own grandchildren may feel rather different. The positive outcome of investing time in his grandchildren may be a relationship that is both possible and a real joy.

References

1 http://ww2.prospects.ac.uk/cms/ShowPage/Home_page/Labour_market_information/Graduate_Market_Trends/Beyond_the_financial_benefits_of_a_degree__Autumn_05_/p!eXeLcmm

2 www.kent.ac.uk

3 Dunbar, R.I., 'Gossip in evolutionary perspective', *Review of General Psychology*, 2004; 8: 100–10

4 http://www.fpa.org.uk/factsheets/teenagers-sexual-health-behaviour

5 Chatav, Y., Coop Gordon, K., Whisman, M., 'Predicting sexual infidelity in a population-based sample of married individuals', *Journal of Family Psychology*, 2007; 21(2): 320–4

6 Susan Krauss Whitbourne, PhD, quoted on www.psychologytoday.com/blog/fulfillment-any-age/201209/the-eight-reasons-people-cheat-their-partners

7 Health and Social Care Information Centre www.hscic.gov.uk

8 'Adolescent Substance Use: America's #1 Public Health Problem', June 2011, available to download from http://www.casacolumbia.org

9 For information and publications try www.talktofrank.com

10 David Tchilingirian, registered nutritionist, www.nutrinsight.co.uk

11 http://www.nhs.uk/Livewell/fitness/Pages/Howmuchactivity.aspx

12 http://www.cdc.gov/features/sleep

13 www.drinkaware.co.uk

14 www.bacp.co.uk

15 www.lifecoach-directory.org.uk

16 http://uk.answers.yahoo.com
17 Couch surfing is a method of finding accommodation while travelling. Couch surfers advertise on the Web, and travellers may stay for free but are expected to return the compliment.
18 Information taken from the British Pregnancy Advisory Sevice (BPAS) website, www.bpas.org

Resources

FOOD, COOKING AND NUTRITION

www.nutrition.org.uk: information and advice on a range of nutritional needs with links to research, publications and training. A healthy-living section includes advice and guidelines for children and adults from birth to older age.

BBC Good Food, www.bbcgoodfood.com/recipes/collection/easy: the BBC's site has easy recipes for those learning to cook.

Student Cooking TV, www.studentcooking.tv: a student cookery site endorsed by many of the key UK universities – with competitions and prizes.

SEXUAL HEALTH

FPA, www.fpa.org.uk: information on sexually transmitted infections, contraception and local services, including sexual assault referral centres.

Brook (for the under 25s), www.brook.org.uk

DRUGS AND ALCOHOL

Frank, www.talktofrank.com: information on drugs – their effects and risks, substances being taken and case studies of usage. The site also offers live chat, information for parents, treatment and support agencies, and the option to text a question, 24 hours a day to 82111.

Drugscope, www.drugscope.org.uk: specialists in research, background, good practice, information service and facts.

Drinkaware, www.drinkaware.co.uk: information and advice on alcohol. There are tips for parents in talking to their young people about alcohol and enabling self-checking of drinking habits.

GENERAL HEALTH
FOR WOMEN

NHS Choices, http://www.nhs.uk/livewell/women4060/Pages/Women 4060home.aspx: health advice specifically for 40- to 60-year-old women with fact sheets and discussions on a wide range of topics, including advice on losing weight, increasing fitness and stopping smoking, etc.

GENERAL HEALTH FOR MEN

NHS Choices, http://www.nhs.uk/chq/pages/category.aspx?Category ID=61: coverage of a wide range of topics with links to information on sexual function problems and paternity tests.

MENTAL HEALTH

MIND, www.mind.org.uk: information on mental health problems, drugs and treatments, helplines and services, groups, rights, tips and guides.

Mental Health Foundation, www.mentalhealth.org.uk: stress support, eating disorders and a range of other topics.

The Student Room, www.thestudentroom.co.uk: chat forums for students on a range of topics, including mental health.

NHS Choices, http://www.nhs.uk/Livewell/studenthealth/Pages/Mentalhealth.aspx: information and links for students on general mental health issues as well as specifics such as drugs and alcohol, food and fitness, etc.

INTERNET ADDICTION

For information and self-help see http://www.helpguide.org/mental/internet_cybersex_addiction.htm

To find a local CBT (Cognitive Behavioural Therapy) practitioner or counsellor: http://www.cbtregisteruk.com/Default.aspx

To find a local accredited therapist or counsellor: www.bacp.co.uk

MONEY AND FINANCES

The Money Advice Service, www.moneyadviceservice.org.uk: independent financial advice, including budget planning, problems with debt, help to rearrange and manage finances, student advice and life event management. The site includes helpful tools such as letter templates and comparison tables. Free printed guides are also available.

CAREERS ADVICE

Connexions (Career support and advice for young people): each area will have its own Connexions service. Your local council should have a link or try Google.

For Connexions Direct, national careers help for 13–19-year-olds with web, chat, text and phone options go to https://www.cxdirect.com/home.htm

The National Careers Service offers step by step support in writing a CV and covering letter, filling in application forms etc. https://nationalcareersservice.direct.gov.uk/advice/getajob/cvs/Pages/default.aspx

For university careers advice go to the individual university website; almost all universities have them.

DOMESTIC VIOLENCE

Domestic Violence Helpline, www.nationaldomesticviolencehelpline.org.uk: for individuals experiencing domestic violence or for friends and family members concerned about someone they know.

TELEPHONE HELPLINES

Sexual Health

Sexual-health helplines offer confidential information and advice (and provide booklets) on:

- contraception methods
- common sexually transmitted infections
- sexuality concerns
- pregnancy choices, abortion and planning a pregnancy

As well as:

- contraception clinics
- sexual health and genitourinary medicine (GUM) clinics
- sexual assault referral centres

FPA sexual-health helpline: 0845 122 8690, 9.00 am to 3.00 pm
Monday to Thursday, 9.00 am to midday Friday.

Ask Brook (up to 25 years old): 0808 802 1234

Drugs
Frank: 0300 123 6600, 24-hour 'talk to someone' line, 24-hour
text service, 82111.

Mental health
Mind Infoline for information on services, help available and
treatments, etc.: 0300 123 3393.

Crisis support
Samaritans: 08457 909090.

Domestic Violence Helpline: 0808 2000 247, a 24-hour national
domestic violence freephone helpline.

Index